CANCER MUST DIE

MY FAITH ADVENTURE

GREG VAN GORP

CANCER MUST DIE

MY FAITH ADVENTURE

GREG VAN GORP

Lithonia, GA

© 2020 Greg Van Gorp
All rights reserved.

No part of this publication may be reproduced, stored in a retrieval system or transmitted in any form or by any means, electronic, mechanical, photocopying, recording or otherwise, without the expressed written permission of the publisher.

Scripture references are taken primarily from the King James Version of the Holy Bible; other versions are also used.
Pronouns for referring to the Father, Son and Holy Spirit are capitalized intentionally and the words satan and devil are never capitalized.

Publisher:
MEWE, LLC
www.mewellc.com

First Edition
ISBN: 978-1-7334383-7-7

Library of Congress Control Number: 2020904401

Printed in the United States of America.

To my Lord and Savior, Jesus Christ, who sent his Word and healed me and restored me and brought me through every trial and tribulation. He is my El-Shaddai, my All Sufficient One. Hallelujah, Hallelujah, Hallelujah!

To my beautiful wife, partner in faith and best friend, Donna. She has stood by me in the battle and believed in me when it seemed like everyone else had given up on me. Her love brought me through and wouldn't let me quit!

Table of Contents

Acknowledgments ix

Foreword xi

Prelude xiii

Introduction xxi

Chapter 1 - Healing Is in the Atonement 1

Chapter 2 - Breaking the Power of Python 9

Chapter 3 - Faith Confrontations 21

Chapter 4 – From the Cross Down.. 29

Chapter 5 - When Our Faith Fails, God Still Works (Pt. 1)... 41

Chapter 6 - When Our Faith Fails, God Still Works (Pt. 2)... 53

Chapter 7 - God Will Use the Faith of Others 65

Chapter 8 - Praise God in Your Pain....................................... 73

About the Author 85

Acknowledgments

I want to thank all the members of Harvest Time Church, friends, and local ministers in Savannah, Georgia.

Special thanks to Pastor Rod Parsley and Bishop Donald Battle for all your support and the teaching that framed my faith in God to let me know Christ is the Healer. And for Bishop Brady Jackson and all the love he has given.

And most of all, I want to thank my beautiful wife, Donna, and our four children, Aaron, Victoria, Alivia, and Greg Jr. (and their mates). I thank them for standing with us through thick and thin, their dedication, which was shown in the music ministry, and for making Harvest Time Church what it is today.

FOREWORD

I've had the pleasure of knowing this warrior shepherd and having him at my side for 40 years. We both received the Lord in the same God Storm around 1980. We have seen each other's growth, maturity, battles, hurts, struggles, mistakes, progressions and breakthroughs in the Lord over the years. Sometimes at a distance, but, always close by in heart and prayer. So, having known this man the way I do for as many years as I have, I consider myself to be a true and accurate assessor of his integrity, faith, walk and love for Christ. As well as his love for God's people and the lost. This man is a true warrior for Christ! In a time when so many families are dealing with this disease called cancer, when so many Christians sadly don't believe in miraculous healing for today and still others believe that God is always going to heal the way they want Him to, a fresh word about Almighty God's desire to heal us through the power and authority of the finished cross work and resurrection of His Son Jesus Christ is greatly needed.

The Lord is always trying to wake us up to something. I believe Pastor Greg has gone through this physical trauma, emotional challenge and life uncertainty to be conditioned and positioned to receive a word from the Lord about the power of God's Word, His goodness and active faith. God's Word is called the sword of the Spirit in Ephesians 6:17. God's Word is a sword, a weapon, and a weapon is used to kill an enemy.

God's Son was the Word who became flesh and He destroyed sin and everything that sin brought into this world through His sacrifice on the cross! Including sickness and disease. It's up to us as Christians to attack sin, these strongholds and all of the effects of sin in our world with the truth of God's Word. His sword. Through Christ's victory at the cross the enemy has been destroyed, and everything that he brought into this world must die! Read on and be empowered and equipped to become one of God's warriors and a part of God's Special Opposition Forces!

Apostle Lary Dean, Senior Pastor
Extreme Church

Prelude

Cancer must die. The word "must" according to Google means that cancer is required to, compelled to, obligated to die! In the summer of 2017, my husband had a cough that lasted for months. I had never seen him with something that lasted this long. We had put up our gospel tent for a baby shower and then left it up for the camp meeting. My son and I were helping my husband take the tent down and he fell to his knees gasping for air. Fear gripped us all.

I began to pray that God would reveal what was happening to my husband. I had seen fear on him about church growth, finances and many other things. Even our relationship was affected by this fear, and now his health. I had been telling him to go see the doctor just to see what may be going on. Now, I'm not one who runs to the doctor with every little symptom and neither is he. But I could tell this was deeper than a simple cold. Was our faith up to the challenge?

Finally, we made a doctor's appointment. They took a lung x-ray and saw a little cloud. They diagnosed him with bronchitis and gave him a steroid and an inhaler. The time came for our annual camp meeting, on July 12-14, at Harvest Time Church. We have been pastoring in Savannah, Georgia since the year 2000 and were expecting pastors from several different states. This is an important and exciting time of the year. The steroid the doctor gave Greg had helped carry him through the camp meeting without coughing. The anointing, grace and strength of the Holy Spirit sustained us through the week's event.

After the camp meeting was over and the medicine was gone, he was still weak and coughing again. Unknown to me, he was coughing up blood. He was referred to a lung specialist who performed another x-ray and a biopsy of his lung. The doctor pulled me aside into a private room and said, "Mrs. Van Gorp, your husband has lung cancer. It's in both his lungs between stage three and four." I was in shock! God allowed my Mother, Rose Allen and her husband who had driven us there to comfort me. The body of Christ is so important in these times, too! My evangelist friend Debra Ann Wittenburg had also come but had to run an errand, but she called me just at the right moment to speak encouraging words to me.

"Ok, Doctor I said, "What's the next step?" I asked if they had told my husband yet. They said they hadn't; they wanted to speak to me first. I said, "It would be better if I am with him when you tell him." They were still waiting for him to awaken from the procedure. When I walked in the room, I held his hand and he could tell it wasn't good. But he didn't expect the diagnosis that was about to hit him.

The doctor used medical terminology and finally came out with it. I saw my husband turn chalky white in color. Life seemed to drain from his eyes. Cancer of the lungs! His maternal grandfather had died at a young age of this very thing! And at this time, Greg was only 55 years. old.

I held his hand, looked in his eyes and spoke to the Spirit of God inside him. "If God is for you, who (or what in this case) can stand against you? We'll make it through this." My husband was still in shock. They took him to day surgery the next day and put a port in his chest. This gave them easy access to putting medicine straight into his veins. They gave him MRIs, CAT scans and PET scans – all kinds of tests. In addition to the lungs, there were six spots of cancer in Greg's brain. It was also in his bones and lymph nodes. He had actually fractured a rib turning on a light switch in his bathroom. The oncologist was on vacation, so they had to wait before deciding on the next medical procedures.

The first battle for me was the one the devil played in my mind. "He's going to die, look at your granddaughter: she will never know her Papa!"

Then God spoke to my spirit with boldness, "What do you say?" I heard the Spirit of God say boldly again; "What do you say?" He gave me a scripture. "Life and death are in the power of your tongue." And then He said it again. "What do you say?"

I finally spoke aloud. "LIFE!" I said, "Father I speak, he will live." I chose, at that point, to tell the devil to shut up. Victory was won that day and something shifted in my heart as my spirit gave me strength.

That August was filled with doctors every day. I remember staying up most of the night, right after the diagnosis and praying to God. I was asking Him to reveal to me what I should do. Then, I started surfing websites and came across a treatment called target therapy. It was better for lung cancer patients than chemo. So, when we met the oncologist, I asked about it. "Yes," he said. "I am going to start him out on one. He's a perfect candidate for this newer treatment."

Then they did another MRI of his brain. This was in February. The first MRI he had taken showed six spots. This was three months later, and it was now showing forty! The sugar he had eaten over the holidays was feeding the cancer. It had spread in his brain! So, they radiated his brain. I was praying and he was standing on God's word, Psalm 107:20: "Thank You, Lord, for sending Your Word to heal me and deliver me from my destructions." We would minister and pray with the people in the waiting room before he would get radiated. One couple who was there were former members of our church. Her husband was getting radiation also, so we would minister to one another. Her husband ended up dying four months later.

Again, I had to keep in my spirit, the word – LIFE. Everyone was praying, including Greg's Catholic mother and her church members. Greg's sisters and brother started to text and e-mail him, and at times call him. This had never happened before. I began to see God doing a work of reconciliation with Greg's family. After much prayer, the test results from the MRI and PET scans, which were taken every three months, came back with a different story: no cancer, just scar tissue. No spots on his brain and no tumors in his lungs. We had been doing Facebook videos at our outreach ministry called 'Coffee and Devotion' led by Ravi Singh. We and other pastors and saints were declaring, "Cancer Must Die!" Remembering that word "Must" means cancer is obligated to die. Praise our Lord – Christ the Healer! But this was only the beginning of our faith tale.

Now, 2018 was drawing to a close. Greg had been free of cancer for six months. He was still taking the target therapy medicine, but at a reduced dose. He was doing well anyway. He was working out at the gym three times a week, running the church and preaching every week. He was visiting the sick in the hospitals and texting his church people with encouraging words. During this time both our daughters got married, in 2018. All was well. We celebrated our 31st wedding anniversary on December 27, 2018, dining in downtown in Savannah, Georgia.

In January 2019 we were back at the oncologist. Greg was complaining about numbness in his big right toe and pain in his right hip and lower back. The doctor said that after the MRI and PET scans, there was no sign of cancer, "You're doing great!"

But I had to ask, "Why the pain?"

The doctor said he didn't know. Greg had never had this pain when battling brain, bone, and lung cancer. This was affecting his ability to run around the block and even walk. There was swelling in his limbs. What could this be? The trauma in his back got so bad that he could not walk without being in pain at every step. I didn't know how much pain he really was in. He doesn't complain much. He has always been a hard worker, a good provider. I had seen my husband go to work, when he ran his own construction company before pastoring full-time, with fever, a swollen face from poison ivy and even the flu.

Finally, I called the oncologist and told them he was in a lot of pain and I was getting no sleep because he was getting none. "Something isn't right," I told the doctor. They sent me a hospice person – really?? My husband was having symptoms like locked up bowels, inability to urinate, and hardly being able to walk! I wanted him to go to the hospital! He was sent to a neurologist and urologist – they gave him a personal catheter. Now he was spared of having a toxic bladder; he was urinating but was still in a lot of pain and, finally, he couldn't walk at all. I was giving him over-the-counter pain killers and it wasn't touching his pain! I prayed, "Help, God! I need You to show up!"

Greg did not want to go to hospital but I finally got an appointment with the oncologist. He sent Greg to the hospital when he took one look at him and saw his son Greg Jr. wheeling him in a wheel chair. Greg's legs were swollen and unable to function. Meanwhile I was praying, "Lord, please get him to the hospital and get him the help he needs. This is too much for him and me." This was a different battle than the one with the previous cancer!

It was Thursday March 14 when he was admitted to the hospital, my oldest daughter's birthday. The medical staff at the hospital did not know the reason for my husband's condition. We were given a semi-private room. The man in the adjoining bed was discharged fifteen minutes after our arrival. They had blocked the room from any other patient because they thought my husband might have contracted aids! They were testing Greg for everything.

I remember how frustrated I was when we got to the hospital because they would not give Greg any pain killer. They said it had to be prescribed by a doctor and he had not been seen yet. Greg was in so much pain, he wasn't making sense even with me anymore. He was talking out of his head. It was so hard for me to watch this going on. At this time my mother-in-law came on her yearly spring visit from Chicago. She wanted to see him in the hospital. Even though I was exhausted from sleeping at the hospital, I felt compelled to be there, so I could hear the doctor's reports in the early morning hours. I asked Greg's mother and Greg Jr. to go to our house and get some sleep. We would rotate. The following night I went home and cried out, "Please, God, show me what's wrong with my husband."

That night I had a dream. I was standing above a brick wall looking down. I saw what looked like four men dressed in casual clothes speaking together in a group. I could tell that one of the men in the group was bald; he was the leader. Then, all of the sudden, in my spirit I recognized these were not men, but demons in men's clothing. My spirit rose up with boldness. I jumped off the wall, landing in front of the bald one. I grabbed the demon by the shirt collar and said, "You have no authority over my husband! The blood of Jesus stands against you, satan! We were standing eye to eye; I saw rage and hate in the demon's eyes. They were blood red. I could tell they were angry at my words, but they were powerless against me. Then I woke up.

What surprised me in the dream were the demons posing as men. Normally, when I have these encounters or dreams, I see these demons as the ugly creatures they have become. So I asked Abba Father, "What does this mean?"

The Holy Spirit spoke to me, "The enemy is going undercover or in disguise in your husband's body. He must be exposed. Pray for the secret things to be exposed" (Luke 8:17; Daniel 2:22; 1 Corinthians 4:5). I called my Intercessors to be in agreement with me in this prayer.

My husband had been in four days of test after test and the doctors still did not know why he was in so much pain nor why nothing was functioning from his waist down. I had faith that something was about to be exposed. The breakthrough came as dear friends, Bishop Brady Jackson and Evangelist Ken Hester, came from Kings Mt. NC. They came for one night to sit with us in the hospital and pray. It was a Sunday night. The doctor did a lumber puncture on Greg's lower spine where the pain was. They had taken a CAT scan of his pelvis only a few weeks earlier. But with this test they saw a mass of growth tangled around his nerves and spinal cord in his lumbar (lower back). The next morning a doctor came in and asked my husband several questions about the type of symptoms he was feeling. My husband confirmed that this was what he had been experiencing. Then they named a specific type of spinal cancer.

People die from this type of cancer in three or four months. The neurologist said that it likes to travel up the spine to the brain. He said Greg would never walk again because of the nerve damage.

OH, BUT REMEMBER GOD! Christ is the Healer! Praise God it was exposed! Now it's war! He loves to show His strength against the impossibilities of life. Greg spent several days in radiation and rehabilitation. However, before returning home he had met his goal of walking 600 steps.

Dear Reader, my prayer to you is that you Stand on God's promises. I found comfort in Psalm 23 every day for weeks, while I drove back and forth daily to the hospital. This scripture brought great strength during my emotional, physical and spiritual tests. Remember, my friend, God will test the word He has put in you as He did with Joseph (Psalm 105:17-22). I came to realize, "This is only a test!" You will pass through this and become stronger and wiser than before.

I believe this book *Cancer Must Die, My Faith Adventure* by my husband, will give you the determination to fight the good fight of faith. This is not just another book! It's a testament of the greatness of our Creator, our Healer, who knows us all so well! Open your heart to His tender hand and allow Him to mold you into an amazing person for Him. Be encompassed by His endless love! Enjoy the Adventure!

Donna Van Gorp

Introduction

Jesus Christ, our great Commander-in-Chief, has already won the battle on our behalf! It's time to walk in His victory. This means all the victory, the power, and the blessing of God is coming toward us all the time and all we have to do is to receive what He has already done. Jesus didn't leave anything undone on the Cross. He finished the work. In saying that, this generation has not seen the miracles, signs, and wonders that previous generations have seen. Even though I have personally seen God do some great miracles, I have not seen the magnitude of past healing revivals such as in the days of A. A. Allen, William Branham, Jack Coe or T. L. Osborn.

All the same, I have seen and experienced powerful miracles and mighty moves of God. I was at Rod Parsley's Dominion camp-meeting and R. W. Schambach was preaching at the afternoon session. When he was done, he laid hands on everyone in the building. I truly believe I received a special anointing that day. I was scheduled to go to Indiana for a healing revival with fellow evangelist Walt Sparks.

During the first night of this revival, the Spirit of God was on the move. A young man was sitting on the right side of the building and I said to him: "You're called to preach, aren't you?" Later he came up for prayer. As we laid hands on him, I said, "I can see the lightnings of God." He took a deep breath and said, "I can breathe, I can breathe." The young man had asthma. God healed him that night in the midst of the revival! Walt got called to go back to Georgia because someone in his church had passed away. I was left with my son Aaron to run the revival.

The following night an older woman came up for healing using a walker. But after the prayer of faith was prayed for her, she went back to her seat dragging that walker behind her. I believe God healed and strengthened her hips and lower body. Christ is the same today as He was yesterday. He is a mighty and awesome God.

We left Indiana and took that anointing to Kentucky. When we got there, we found out the church we were visiting was about ready to be shut down because rock slides had caused tremendous damage to the roads and the City had to block the only road that led to the church in order to fix the problem. Right before we got there the project was completed and the road reopened. God does amazing things.

The first night of preaching, an older woman came up to me and said, "I can't see." I laid hands on her eyes and prayed the prayer of faith. When I was done, I looked at her and she took off her glasses. Then she looked around, and still said, "I can't see." So, I prayed again with the same results. At this point, I looked up to Heaven and the Holy Spirit said, "Spit on the eyes." I thought, *yuck* as a picture of spittle entered my mind. Then I put my thumbs to my tongue and laid them on her eyes for the third time. This time she said, "I can see!"

Later that night I prayed for a deaf woman. I put my fingers in her ears three times, with the same results. She walked back to her seat the same way she came up. After service, the pastor took us out to dinner. He received a phone call while we were out and, to my surprise, the deaf woman I prayed for was the pastor's sister. She told him, "I can hear a dial tone in my deaf ear for the first time in my life!"

God is a healer! Numbers 23:19 states, *"God is not a man, that he should lie; neither the son of man, that he should repent: hath he said, and shall he not do it? or hath he spoken, and shall he not make it good?"* He's a good God!

Pastor Greg Van Gorp

HEALING IS IN THE ATONEMENT

As Christians, we believe and have confidence that Jesus died for our sicknesses as well as our sins, and that physical healing is provided for in the atoning work of Christ on the Cross. Therefore, healing is in the atonement, meaning when Jesus paid for our sins, He paid for our healing! Hebrews 13:8 states, *"Jesus Christ is the same yesterday, today, and forever."* That means if He healed in the Old Covenant, He will heal in the New Covenant. If He prospered you in the old Covenant, He will prosper you in the new Covenant. What He was, He is. He is a Healer. He has risen from the dead!!! Isaiah 53:4-5 states, *"Surely he hath borne our griefs and carried our sorrows: yet we did esteem him stricken, smitten of God, and afflicted. But he was wounded for our transgressions, he was bruised for our iniquities: the chastisement of our peace was upon him, and with his stripes we are healed."* This scripture clearly states that by His stripes we are healed. The word "are" is a present participle, meaning it is still active in our reality now! It was done when Jesus was scourged at the whipping post and it is still efficacious today.

Purged of Guilt

It would be a very prideful thing for me to reject the healing which Jesus has purchased at such a cost. I do believe that the main thing that holds back healing is a guilty conscience, but according to Hebrews 9:14, *"How much more shall the blood of Christ, who through the eternal Spirit offered himself without spot to God, purge your conscience from dead works to serve the living God."*

Here we see that Christ offered Himself; no one made Him do it. He laid down His will and obeyed His heavenly Father's will! The reason was to "purge your conscience from dead works." What a statement! The guilt, the shame, the pride is gone, the works of the flesh eradicated. How? We receive it by faith! The blood of Jesus sets us free!

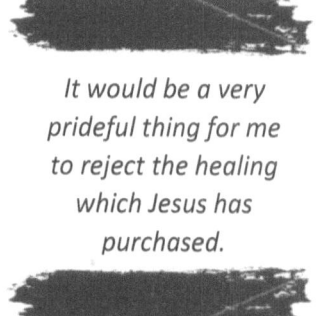

It would be a very prideful thing for me to reject the healing which Jesus has purchased.

The parallel scripture is found in Hebrews 10:19-22:

Having therefore, brethren, boldness to enter into the holiest by the blood of Jesus, by a new and living way, which he hath consecrated for us, through the veil, that is to say, his flesh. And having a high priest over the house of God; Let us draw near with a true heart in full assurance of faith, having our hearts sprinkled from an evil conscience, and our bodies washed with pure water.

Notice that the scripture says our hearts have been sprinkled from an evil conscience. When we receive by faith the washing of our conscience, we can receive God's healing.

The new way is through the sacrifice of the flesh of Jesus Christ. Christ's flesh was torn not one time, but seven times. He bled in the garden, He bled when the crown of thorns was driven into His head, He bled at the scourging at the whipping post, He bled in His hands, His feet, and His side when His heart was pierced, and He was bruised for our transgressions. When He died, the veil which separated the Holy Place from the Holy of Holies was torn from top to bottom, not bottom to top. It's all about God coming down to meet man because the sacrifice has been made for Adam's sin.

He Is Our Provider

Back when my son Aaron was eleven years old, right before he turned twelve, I was out of work as a carpenter. Well, when you can't feed your family, it's a good time to fast. So I went on a four day fast. Aaron asked, "Dad, can I go on the fast with you?" to which I responded, "Sure!" However, I wondered how long the kid would last without food. Well, Aaron is pretty tough and lasted the entire four days.

I went out looking for work. The first thing I did was to go to the unemployment center. I heard the Holy Spirit say to my spirit, "This is a waste of time." He was right, so I drove up East Broad Street in Savannah, Georgia, and saw a group of carpenters. Right then it started to rain and I said to myself, *I'm weak from fasting, I'll talk to them tomorrow*. Again, the Holy Spirit spoke to my heart and said, 'NO! Do it now!'

So, I got out of my vehicle and went up to the man at the carpenter's desk, who just happened to be the foreman, and I asked, "Are you looking for any carpenters?" He replied, "That's amazing, I just had one quit." He took me into the house and showed me where a multi-level staircase was to be and asked if I could build that. I said, "I believe I can." "Great," he responded, "You start Monday." I went straight to Home Depot and bought a book on how to build stairs.

After building the stairs, I built the railing, the chair rail and the wainscoting, and then finished off with the crown molding on the second floor. Later, I installed a metal roof to an addition they had built. To me, this was important because, when the doctor told me I had cancer, I bought a book called **The One Minute Cure** by Madison Cavanaugh. In this book, it tells you how to take food grade hydrogen peroxide. At that time, I was standing on the Word of God in Psalm 107:20-21 that states, *"He sent his word, and healed them, and delivered them from their destructions. Oh that men would praise the Lord for his goodness, and for his wonderful works to the children of men!"* God is a good God and He will do great things for you, if you trust Him.

There are three types of jobs you can get in life. The worldly job, which works you till you drop. Then there are self-jobs. Here you work a little bit and you make some money. Lastly, there are God jobs. With God jobs, you work a little and you make a whole lot. It is the work of ministry.

In Luke 5, Jesus told Peter to let out his net for a catch even though Peter had worked all night and caught nothing. Peter obeyed and caught a great multitude of fish. This was his business. For the next three years we know he traveled with Jesus.

The lady whose dream home I was working on had a sick iguana. She found out I was a minister and had me pray for the iguana. I prayed really hard for it to get healed. I thought if God healed the iguana, the lady would get saved. Unfortunately, the iguana died, but the lady gave her heart to Jesus anyway. God will make a way where there is no way.

New Kid on the Block

Aaron stayed on the fast and adjusted it to a partial fast. I can remember coming home from work one day, saying, "Aaron, what did you have to eat today?" He replied, "Daddy, I didn't have anything to eat today." I asked, "What did you have to drink today?" He said, "Daddy, I can't remember if I took a drink." After this, Donna and I began to monitor Aaron in a much closer way. He stayed on that fast for about a year.

During this time, we were invited to a revival and the Evangelist we were working with called Evangelist Van Gorp up to the pulpit. Aaron and I both asked, "Which one?"

The Evangelist said, "Sit down, old man, we want to hear from the kid!"

Aaron went up to the pulpit and the Evangelist sat him down in a chair on the stage. The chair was right by the speaker and I knew that was not good. The Evangelist felt it, too, because he did not give the microphone to Aaron. So, we left after the meeting and I thought that was it. The following day, a Saturday, we were downtown shopping with the family. I am not a fan of Saturday shopping and usually when I am done, it's home to rest.

The voice of the Holy Spirit went off in my spirit and said, "Tonight is Aaron's night." I told my wife and the family, and I went home to get ready, expecting God to move. By the time we were ready and got to the church, the place was packed. Praise and worship had ended and the Evangelist had been given the microphone. He started to preach and then stopped. He was looking around for Aaron; he located him and called him to the platform. He said to Aaron, "I'm going to hand you this microphone and you can do whatever you want.

You can preach, teach, pray, sing, pray in tongues, whatever you want to do." Now, Aaron was a very small eleven-year-old and he had been fasting, so he was very skinny. He handed the microphone to Aaron and the Holy Spirit hit Aaron. He let out a strong and bold "Glory to God, everybody." Immediately the entire church was electrified with the power of God.

Aaron had been listening to his father's preaching and began to preach about how the veil of the temple was torn from top to bottom, and not from bottom to top when Jesus died. He handed the microphone back to the Evangelist, who tried to preach, but gave the microphone back to Aaron. Aaron preached for a few more minutes and handed it back to the Evangelist. He then took Aaron's hand and put it in his coat pocket and said, "Keep this right there." As they did the altar call, the power of God fell and people were completely healed and delivered. As the veil was torn, so was Jesus' flesh torn for our healing, in the atonement.

The Lord will take away from thee all sickness...

He Bore Our Sicknesses and Sorrows

Dr. T. J. McCrossen in his book, *Bodily Healing and the Atonement,* referenced Isaiah 53:4, *"Surely he [Christ] hath borne our griefs [kholee, sicknesses H2483], and carried our sorrows [makob, pains H4341]."*

Kholee (sickness) is from challah [H2470], to be weak, sick, or afflicted. In Deuteronomy 7:15 we read, *"The Lord will take away from thee all sickness [kholee]."* This word is translated as "sickness" in Deuteronomy 28:61, 1 Kings 17:17, 2 Kings 1:2, 2 Kings 8:8, and other places.

Makob is translated "pain" in Job 33:19, "*He is chastened also with pain [makob].*" In Jeremiah 51:8 we read, "*Take balm for her pain [makob].*" Then Isaiah 53:4 should read, "Surely he [Christ] hath borne our sicknesses, and carried our pains." Every impartial Hebrew scholar must admit that this is the correct translation.

Let us now examine the verbs in Isaiah 53:4, "borne" (nasa) and "carried" (sabal). (1.a) The Hebrew verb nasa [H5375] means to bear in the sense of "suffering punishment for something." Leviticus 5:1, "*And if a soul sin ... then he shall bear [nasa] his iniquity.*" In Isaiah 53:12, we have the true meaning of nasa: set forth: "*And he [Christ] was numbered with the transgressors; and he bare [nasa] the sin of many*".

Now how did Christ bear our sins? Vicariously, as our substitute. But this is the same verb used in Isaiah 53:4, "*Surely he [Christ] hath borne [nasa] our sicknesses.*"

We all admit that this verb (nasa) in Isaiah 53:12 teaches us that Christ bore our sins vicariously; so all unprejudiced minds must admit that this very same verb (nasa) in Isaiah 53:4 teaches us that He {Christ} bore our sicknesses vicariously. Yes, the very same verb (nasa) is used of bearing our sins in Isaiah 53:12 as is used in Isaiah 53:4 of bearing our sicknesses. The clear teaching, therefore, is that Christ bore our sicknesses in the very same way that He bore our sins. There can be no other conclusion. What an awesome word! The same way we receive salvation is the same way we receive healing – by faith!

BREAKING THE POWER OF PYTHON

Every year I go into a time of prayer and God gives me the word for that year. In 2019 it was "Releasing Heaven's Inheritance." The Holy Spirit told me, "Sanctify yourself (Joshua 3:5), for you have not passed this way heretofore." Deuteronomy 2:3 states: "*Ye have compassed this mountain long enough: turn you northward.*" North is always a representation of Heaven. It's time to live life for Heaven's eternity! When you do this, a couple things will happen. As a result of your sanctification, God will work wonders in your life and God will magnify His plans and His purposes in you (See Joshua 3:5).

Verse eight states you shall command the priests to bear the Ark. This is the Ark of the Covenant. It sat in the Holy of Holies behind the Veil in the Tabernacle. It was a wooden box covered in Gold with two angels. The angels sat on top of the box, arching their wings over the middle of the box which is called the Mercy Seat. The Shekinah Glory, the actual presence of God, sat on that box. The priests were to carry the presence of God! We, as born again believers, are to carry the presence of God! He builds His temple in us. This is not to take away from the church and the gathering of the saints together. God loves it when the saints get together. *"And let them make me a sanctuary; that I may dwell among them"* (Exodus 25:8).

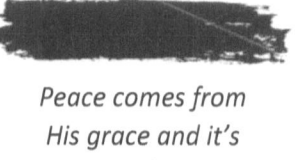

Peace comes from His grace and it's where there is nothing missing and nothing broken...

God's plan and purpose is to dwell among you and in you as He does corporately in the church body. How is this done? By the Holy Spirit. God has a vision. God has a plan and His plan is to manifest His kingdom in you! To do this, He gives you grace and peace. Grace is God's unmerited favor. Peace comes from His grace and it's where there is nothing missing and nothing broken in your life. God loves you and He is concerned about your life.

His Virtue Is Within You

> *Grace and peace be multiplied unto you through the knowledge of God, and of Jesus our Lord, According as his divine power hath given unto us all things that pertain unto life and godliness, through the knowledge of him that hath called us to glory and virtue: Whereby are given unto us exceeding great and precious promises: that by these ye might be partakers of the divine nature, having escaped the corruption that is in the world through lust* (2 Peter 1:2-4).

Some amazing things are stated in this portion of scripture. It's God's will that we are partners of His Divine nature! What a statement! In order to accomplish this, He has called us to experience His glory. The glory of God rests on you; the virtue of God resides in you.

A very famous story is recorded in Mark 5:24-34. It's the story of the woman with the issue of blood.

> *And a certain woman, which had an issue of blood twelve years, And had suffered many things of many physicians, and had spent all that she had, and was nothing bettered, but rather grew worse, When she had heard of Jesus, came in the press behind, and touched his garment. For she said,' If I may touch but his clothes, I shall be whole.' And straightway the fountain of her blood was dried up; and she felt in her body that she was healed of that plague. And Jesus, immediately knowing in himself that virtue had gone out of him, turned him about in the press, and said, 'Who touched my clothes?'*

I noticed a few things about this woman that amazed me. The first thing is that she had desperate faith. Desperate, determined faith is mountain-moving faith. Romans 10:17 says, *"So then faith cometh by hearing, and hearing by the word of God."* She heard about Jesus and pressed her way in and spoke faith within herself. You've got to speak faith! In speaking faith, she painted a picture of healing within herself. Because she had an issue of blood, she should have been announcing "unclean" as she passed through the massive crowd. But the Father, the Son and the Holy Spirit respond to faith. When she touched Jesus' garment, she drew the power or virtue right out of Him. Jesus wanted everyone to know that it was not simply the touching of His garments that resulted in her being healed, but it was the intensity of her faith.

The world is desperate for this kind of anointing, for this kind of operation in the Spirit. I believe she took the Lord by surprise! Jesus said, "Who touched me?" He could feel the power, the virtue leave His body. Oh, how I crave to know and love God like that! To have the power of God rest within me and know it. I am desperate to hold on to such anointing.

This woman purposed in her heart, "If I can touch Him, I will be made whole!" She did it. Faith involves an act and she acted on her faith. When she confessed that she was healed, she locked it in, and then she went and acted on it. I firmly believe that the absence of faith would not have resulted in her healing.

Your testimony of God's miracles in your life locks in what He has done for you! That's why I tell everyone about Psalm 107:20, "He sent his word and healed me and delivered me from all destructions." God said it, I believe it and that settles it. I'm healed by the stripes of Jesus.

A friend of mine asked that we go pray for his Dad who was battling cancer. This was in the early 2000s and we had just started ministry in downtown Savannah, Georgia. He picked me up and we went to his father's house. When we got there, his mother had some of the best cornbread and veggie soup I'd ever eaten. We prayed the prayer of faith laying hands on his father. I could feel a tingle pass through my hands as we prayed! On the way home, I felt them burn with the power of God. My friend parked in the driveway, I grabbed his hand and he could feel it too. The following Sunday he came to church and told me, "The doctor can't find any cancer in my father's body."

Hallelujah! That's the virtue, the resurrection power of Jesus Christ at work. He is Lord over all. He has power over cancer, and all forms of sickness. They must all die in His presence. Joshua 3:5 states, *"And Joshua said unto the people, Sanctify yourselves: for to morrow the LORD will do wonders among you."* Here God was doing something in the natural for the children of Israel. What He is doing for the church today is getting us out of the flesh and into the Spirit. And that's what a Priest does for his congregation: he stands in the gap on their behalf.

> *And Aaron shall bear the names of the children of Israel in the breastplate of judgment upon his heart, when he goeth in unto the holy place, for a memorial before the Lord continually. And thou shalt put in the breastplate of judgment the Urim and the Thummim; and they shall be upon Aaron's heart, when he goeth in before the Lord: and Aaron shall bear the judgment of the children of Israel upon his heart before the Lord continually* (Exodus 28:29-30).

Notice here the breastplate of judgment is upon Aaron's heart when he goes before the Lord. That same judgment was laid upon Jesus. His priestly office is expounded in the book of Hebrews. But I also like what it says in James 5:13-16:

> *Is any among you afflicted? let him pray. Is any merry? let him sing psalms. Is any sick among you? let him call for the elders of the church; and let them pray over him, anointing him with oil in the name of the Lord: And the prayer of faith shall save the sick, and the Lord shall raise him up; and if he have committed sins, they shall be forgiven him. Confess your faults one to another, and pray one for another, that ye may be healed. The effectual fervent prayer of a righteous man availeth much.*

In this passage of scripture, James makes a distinction between the sick and the afflicted. He says the sick should call for the elders of the church to pray, but the one who is afflicted is to pray for himself. Here he is teaching that whatever your situation is, you are to respond to it with prayer. Then he went on to ask, "Is any merry?" Why would he say that in the middle of dealing with the sick and afflicted? I believe James is saying here that, regardless of our circumstances, we are to pray. Not only when we are sick or experiencing affliction, but even when we are prospering in all aspects of life, we are to be thankful to God for His many blessings.

I believe in the power of prayer. Back in 1982, I was managing a rock band called Trytan, in the Chicago area and one of the young men, hanging around the band invited me to a benefit concert for someone who was dying of cancer. When we got there, the bands were switching over and I told my friend, "It would be great if someone could go up on stage and pray for the guy."

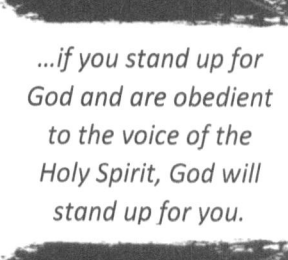

...if you stand up for God and are obedient to the voice of the Holy Spirit, God will stand up for you.

He asked me, "Do you want to do that?"

I said, "What will I say?"

He showed me James 5, how the prayer of faith shall save the sick, and the Lord shall raise him up.

I was a 20-year-old with long hair, wearing my Dad's marine field jacket. With that I walked onto the stage, took the microphone and prayed. People in the crowd started heckling. But when I walked off stage, something happened that I didn't expect: the people applauded. That's when I learned, if you stand up for God and are obedient to the voice of the Holy Spirit, God will stand up for you.

Defeating the Python Spirit

God took me to Acts 16:16-40. In this passage of Scripture, Paul and Silas are just minding their own business going to prayer! Their mission was to fulfill the vision God gave them in Acts 16:9,10. The people of Macedonia didn't know they needed help – but God did.

A lot of times in life, we don't realize how much we need God. There is a major spiritual confrontation getting ready to take place where principalities and powers of this darkened world will be overthrown. That same power is available today for you and me.

> *And it came to pass, as we went to prayer, a certain damsel possessed with a spirit of divination met us, which brought her masters much gain by soothsaying: The same followed Paul and us, and cried, saying, These men are the servants of the most high God, which shew unto us the way of salvation. And this did she many days. But Paul, being grieved, turned and said to the spirit, I command thee in the name of Jesus Christ to come out of her. And he came out the same hour* (Acts 16:16-18).

In Finis Jennings *Dake's Annotated Reference Bible* it states, referring to the spirit of divination, "Gr. Spirit of python, or Apollo. Python, was according to fable, a huge serpent that had an oracle on Mt. Parnassus, famous for predicting future events. Apollo slew this serpent and was called Pythius. He became celebrated as the foreteller of events. It was believed that all who pretended to foretell events were influenced by the spirit of Apollo Pythius. A Priestess at his temple was called Pythoness. Through her, messages were delivered."

We can see that this young woman spoke forth demonically inspired messages and made her masters a lot of money. It sounded good, she looked good, and the people exalted her. If you needed help, you went to her for answers. The Apostles were going to prayer. This Python devil's primary assignment is to keep the church from praying. Now, here is something really amazing. This devil is masquerading as the church. The girl says, *"These men are the servants of the most high God, which shew unto us the way of salvation."* Wow, the witch has a good report? She's saying the right thing, but she has the wrong spirit.

When Donna and I graduated from World Harvest Bible College, we were looking for the place that God was calling us to start a church. We had visited Donna's friend in South Carolina and God orchestrated events with a woman and her husband that I had taught in a new believers' class at World Harvest Church. We drove from Charleston, S.C. and entered Georgia. As we came over the Talmadge Memorial Bridge, God spoke. He said, "I'm calling you to a people you do not know, trapped in bondage of a slave mentality brought in by a spirit of VooDoo." VooDoo, witchcraft, tarot card reading, they are all from the devil, and when we pulled into Savannah, Georgia, it was easy to see that Python, the spirit of divination, false prophecy, was the ruling spirit there.

The Python kills its victims differently than other snakes. Non-poisonous snakes kill their victims by swallowing them. Poisonous snakes kill their victims by biting them and injecting venom into them. God is a good, gracious and kind God, and He watches out for you and your children.

When my children were little and we first moved to Savannah, Georgia, I told them to always wear boots when going through the woods. There was a nice wooded area right behind my house, and across the street our neighbors had a pond. One day the kids came into the house yelling, "Snake! Snake!" They had seen a water moccasin coming out of the pond and crossing the street. I ran and got the spade. Snakes, like cancer, have to die. I cut its head off with the shovel.

I had a similar situation happen not long after that. My youngest daughter, Alivia, is an animal lover and she loves her dogs. So unknown to me, she was taking her dogs for a run in the woods. Was she wearing boots? Of course not, in Georgia. Flip flops! The kids come running into the house yelling, "Snake! Snake!" and saying the dog saw it and jumped out of the way. I loved that stray dog from that day on! Again, I grabbed the shovel, went after the snake. It was a large diamond-back and I killed it. After that, all I could do was praise God! He had protected my children once again. He is always watching over us. When I was diagnosed with cancer, dying was the furthest thing from my mind. I knew Jesus had already killed that snake!

As I said before, the Python kills its victims differently than other snakes. It ambushes you by positioning itself in a high place, jumps out and strikes you with its teeth, then coils and suffocates the life out of you. When you are dealing with the spirit of Python, you are not dealing with a low level devil. Python works closely with Beelzebub, Lord of the Flies. It's not one thing that takes a Christian out, it is usually a series of things working behind the scenes, bringing confusion. One fly then another, then another, until they are swarming and the Christian can't see their way out. The enemy is trying to distract you from your purpose, completely consuming you with pointless battles to make you weary and deactivate your focus. Finally, you give up. Beelzebub will position the Christian under the Python spirit which seemingly drops out of nowhere and begins to coil itself around the victim's body. So every time the victim tries to take a breath, it squeezes just a little bit tighter until the victim can't catch their breath.

We have to understand that this is the end-time spirit's mission to attack the church. This spirit is after the breath (*ruach*) of God, the wind of God. In Acts 2, we are told there was a mighty rushing wind. The church was born and the power of God was released. The Pharisees accused Jesus of casting out demons with the spirit of…look what Jesus reveals to them.

> *Then was brought unto him one possessed with a devil, blind, and dumb: and he healed him, insomuch that the blind and dumb both spake and saw. And all the people were amazed, and said, Is not this the son of David? But when the Pharisees heard it, they said, This fellow doth not cast out devils, but by Beelzebub the prince of the devils.*
>
> *And Jesus knew their thoughts, and said unto them, Every kingdom divided against itself is brought to desolation; and every city or house divided against itself shall not stand: And if Satan cast out Satan, he is divided against himself; how shall then his kingdom stand? And if I by Beelzebub cast out devils, by whom do your children cast them out? therefore they shall be your judges. But if I cast out devils by the Spirit of God, then the kingdom of God is come unto you. Or else how can one enter into a strong man's house, and spoil his goods, except he first*

bind the strong man? and then he will spoil his house. He that is not with me is against me; and he that gathereth not with me scattereth abroad. (Matthew 12:22-30).

You are either for Christ or against Him.

How does a Spirit-filled Christian cast out devils? The same way Jesus did it: by the Spirit of God. The Holy Spirit united with a faith-filled Bible-believing Christian is the Lord's battle axe. There is an old saying, "She's a real battle axe." In the realm of the Spirit, if you have a praying wife, as I do, there's no better battle axe on earth to defeat the work of the devil.

Faith Confrontations

In the Kingdom of God, there are no free rides. People can pray for you, but you have to know God for yourself. My love and knowledge of God, His will and His goodness came through power confrontations. Back in the early 1980s, I was looking for God to move into my life. I was living in the Chicago area where I was raised. I was managing a rock band called Trytan and it was during this time I started reading my Bible. The Spirit of God began to grow in me and I was no longer interested in getting "high" or drinking beer.

My Search

There was an intense battle for my mind going on in the realm of the spirit. I got to a place in my heart where I really wanted to know God. I took a week's vacation from my job, got in my car and drove up to a Catholic Monastery in Wisconsin. I stayed in the woods and just prayed and fasted the best I knew how. I didn't even bring a Bible. I didn't understand the power of God the way I do now. Everything is in the Word, and the

Word works. The following year, I bought a backpack and some camping equipment, and by the time I'd loaded everything into the backpack, I thought it was somewhat heavy, so I put it on the scale. It weighed 109 lbs. But I was young and strong, so I started to hike up to Canada. I was raised Catholic and I fully intended to become a monk like St. Francis of Assisi, but I came to realize that walking up HWY 295 in Chicago was not the best idea. A police officer stopped me a few miles up and told me I was not allowed to walk on this road ending my first Faith Confrontation. But even in your faith failures, God can still use you.

I didn't know what to do, so I went home and shared my heart with my dad. My dad was the typical come-home two-Martini six-pack-of-beer kind of businessman. But one thing I knew for certain, my dad loved me. He gave me some great advice: "Son, go see your uncle Ben." My Uncle Ben was a great man. He was a high school football coach and influenced hundreds of lives. So, I drove up to Wisconsin and shared my heart with him and my aunt Catherine, my father's sister. This was God and I didn't know it but I was on my way to my second Power Confrontation. My uncle took me around to different ministries around Appleton, Wisconsin, where my father is from.

One was called the Rock and we stopped in to see a young man named Bob. Bob said: "We are going to Canton, Ohio, for the NFL Hall of Fame weekend. We are going to share Jesus on the streets. We will stop by Chicago and pick you up." On the day they were coming down, Bob called: "Wait at the corner of Ogden Ave and HWY 295; it will be faster for us."

As I stood waiting at that corner for what I thought would be about ten to fifteen minutes, it started to rain. My mind kept telling me to go home, but my spirit wouldn't let me. After three hours they finally showed up. Thank God, I won that faith confrontation!

I had a great time sharing my faith during the Hall of Fame weekend. I noticed that when I prayed with people on the streets, they straightened up. When you reach outside yourself, the power of God will always show up. The following day, Saturday, the pastor whose church we were visiting took us to a Christian outdoor play called "Trumpet in the Land." I was sitting in my seat minding my own business when the Holy Spirit spoke: "I have a job for you to do down here."

Faith Confrontations

The following day, I was in church and I said to the Lord, "Well, Lord, if I'm not going to be a monk, how about a wife? Sitting about seven rows in front of me was a line of young women and one had beautiful red hair. God said: "That one!!" Well, the group I was with went up to the front of the altar area to sing a song. As they were singing, I was trying to check out this girl. I didn't want an ugly woman. *Thank You, Lord, that one's beautiful,* I thought. Two years later, I moved to Canton, Ohio at the request of the Pastor. The girl was now a woman and engaged to another guy. It was time for another faith confrontation.

We have a key to victory in Acts 13:1-3:

Now there were in the church that was at Antioch certain prophets and teachers; as Barnabas, and Simeon that was called Niger, and Lucius of Cyrene, and Manaen, which had been brought up with Herod the tetrarch, and Saul. As they ministered to the Lord, and fasted, the Holy Ghost said, Separate me Barnabas and Saul for the work whereunto I have called them.

And when they had fasted and prayed, and laid their hands on them, they sent them away.

This was a group of five church leaders. I believe that, if God calls you to start a church, He will also give you five church leaders. The leader of the church here in Acts is Barnabas. The teacher in the group is Saul, but he is last in authority. This is called the law of first mention and how biblical manuscripts are written. Barnabas brought Saul from the Island of Cyprus to teach at the church in Antioch. Because Saul was raised a Pharisee, he knew Jewish customs, could teach Hebrew Law, and could expound the Old Testament scriptures concerning Christ the Messiah. Notice *"they ministered to the Lord and fasted"*! We have lost much of this in the church today. The church doesn't like to fast, and ministering to the Lord is a lost art. But when they did, they heard the voice of God. Isn't that what life is all about – hearing, knowing, receiving and loving God? Loving God and hearing His voice and obeying Him is what produces good results in life.

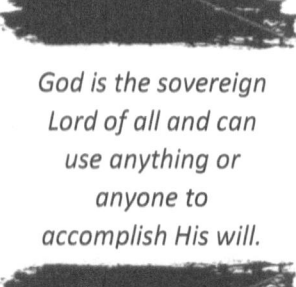

God is the sovereign Lord of all and can use anything or anyone to accomplish His will.

In Acts 13:6 Barnabas and Saul go to the island of Paphos. Here they have not just a faith confrontation, but a power confrontation. They find a sorcerer, a false prophet named Elymas, who withstood them as they preached to the deputy of the country, Sergius Paulus. While Jesus was called to the poor, Paul was called to the heads of state. Everywhere Paul went, he got the leaders in the region saved. Verse 9 is the first time the Bible mentions Saul being called Paul, and he has a prophetic word that causes blindness to come upon the sorcerer.

Paul was familiar with this phenomenon. After Jesus appeared to him on the road to Damascus, he fell from his horse and was blind for three days until Ananias laid hands on him. It was a power confrontation and the Lord won. After Paul gave this prophetic word, blindness came on the sorcerer. Through this confrontation, the deputy believed and the Lord won again.

The Book of Acts and the whole Bible is full of power confrontations. During these times, it is very important that you listen to the Holy Spirit. When Ananias goes and lays hands on Saul, Jesus tells him in Acts 9:15, *"Go thy way: for he is a chosen vessel unto me, to bear my name before the Gentiles, and kings, and the children of Israel."*

As a Pharisee, Paul is very familiar with the law of first mention. That means what is stated first by an authority is what you do first. He is called to go to the Gentiles, to kings, and then to the children of Israel. But Paul says in Romans 1:16, *"For I am not ashamed of the gospel of Christ: for it is the power of God unto salvation to every one that believeth; to the Jew first, and also to the Greek."* Notice, Paul has the order reversed. And I have to say this, "God is the sovereign Lord of all and can use anything or anyone to accomplish His will."

In 2 Corinthians 12, Paul talks about a man who has been to the third heaven. I believe there are three heavens. Not ten, but three. The first is our immediate atmosphere where the clouds are, the second is where the sun, moon, and stars are, and the third is where God dwells, and that's where Paul was caught up to. While there, I believe he received those wonderful revelations of who we are in Christ and where we are seated, as spoken of in his prison epistles. And because of these revelations, he was given a thorn in the flesh. 2 Corinthians 12:7-10 states:

> *And lest I should be exalted above measure through the abundance of the revelations, there was given to me a thorn in the flesh, the messenger of satan to buffet me, lest I should be exalted above measure. For this thing I besought the Lord thrice, that it might depart from me. And he said unto me, My grace is sufficient for thee: for my strength is made perfect in weakness. Most gladly therefore will I rather glory in my infirmities, that the power of Christ may rest upon me.*

Therefore, I, too, take pleasure in infirmities, in reproaches, in necessities, in persecutions, in distresses for Christ's sake: for when I am weak, then am I strong.

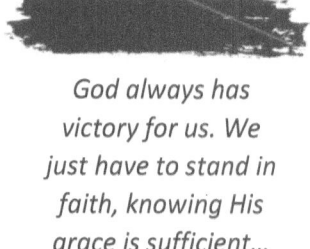

God always has victory for us. We just have to stand in faith, knowing His grace is sufficient...

Paul states that a thorn in the flesh was given to him, the messenger of satan. Here is my question to you: we know that messengers of satan are demons. Would God give Paul a demon? Some scholars say the thorn in the flesh was sickness, but I don't believe that either. The scripture will interpret itself. Numbers 33:55 states, *"But if ye will not drive out the inhabitants of the land from before you; then it shall come to pass, that those which ye let remain of them shall be pricks in your eyes, and thorns in your sides, and shall vex you in the land wherein ye dwell."* Joshua 23:13 states the same thing. Thorns are people the devil sends against you to stop the work of God. I believe it had nothing to do with sickness.

When Paul says a thorn in the flesh was given him, a messenger of satan so he would not be exalted above measure. I believe what he is saying is this: "The Lord took me to the third heaven so He could communicate who we really are in Christ. He sent me to deliver the message, and every time I do, these thorns or people come against me to stop the revelation being given to the church, the revelation of who we are and where we are seated in Christ." About this, Paul said he appealed to the Lord three times and the Lord said, *"My grace is sufficient for thee."* Grace is God's unmerited favor. A thorn in the flesh is not favor and it's not grace. I believe the term *"Lest I should be exalted above measure"* is a reference to the message Paul is preaching and not to Paul himself.

Going back to the law of first mention, the Lord is saying, "Paul, if you do it my way you will have the victory you seek." Paul was called to the Gentiles, kings, and the Jews. In Acts 18:6 he understood, *"And when they opposed themselves, and blasphemed, he shook his raiment, and said unto them, Your blood be upon your own heads; I am clean: from henceforth I will go unto the Gentiles."* Here, Paul finally gets it right and look what happens. Acts 18:9: *"Then spake the Lord to Paul in the night by a vision, Be not afraid, but speak, and hold not thy peace: For I am with thee, and no man shall set on thee to hurt thee: for I have much people in this city."* Paul is going the right way doing the right thing and Jesus is with him and *"no man shall set on thee to hurt thee."*

I believe this is where and how Paul gets the victory over the 'thorn in the flesh.' God always has victory for us. We just have to stand in faith, knowing His grace is sufficient for us.

I had to learn this when I moved from Chicago to Canton, Ohio. It was almost three years after my first visit there when I relocated. The girl God told me I was going to marry was engaged to another guy. The Pastor that I believe God wanted me to train under kept avoiding me. Later he told me every time I got around him, he would get a knot in the pit of his stomach. I asked him why and he said he didn't know.

During this time, I was very confused and distraught – talk about a faith conflict! When I believed what God had told me I would be happy and when I didn't believe or even doubt God, I would become depressed. Finally, I got sick and tired of being depressed and I made the decision in my heart that I'm going to believe what God had told me. I might have to wait until this guy dies, but one day this girl will be my wife. I made that decision and was happy with it. Then my roommate started dating the sister of the girl God told me I was going to marry. I said in my heart, "That's God, I've got this one!"

I was attending Malone Collage at the time and was having classes with the fiancé of the girl God told me I was to marry. My vehicle broke down one day and I had to ask him for a ride home. On the way I thought it would be a good idea to tell him what God had told me and ask him to take good care of Donna because she was my future wife. Donna and I started dating one month later on December 28, 1986. We were married December 27, 1987, and she is by far the greatest blessing I could have ever hoped for.

Real faith will always have confrontations, but if you stick with Jesus and don't grow weary in well doing you will have the victory He's already won and will not experience faith failure.

FROM THE CROSS DOWN

Luke 23:34: *"Then said Jesus, Father, forgive them; for they know not what they do."*

In the eleventh chapter of the Book of Mark, we see Jesus getting ready to go into Jerusalem on His triumphal entry. He tells His disciples to get Him a colt.

> *And saith unto them, Go your way into the village over against you: and as soon as ye be entered into it, ye shall find a colt tied, whereon never man sat; loose him, and bring him. And if any man say unto you, Why do ye this? say ye that the Lord hath need of him; and straightway he will send him hither* (Mark 11:2-3).

Why didn't Jesus have them buy a donkey? Jesus had money. Traveling with twelve apostles takes a lot of money. Judas was the treasurer and he stole money without anyone noticing. The reason is that Jesus knew how to operate in the fullness of the Father's provision.

The Legal term would be called "eminent domain." According to Merriam Webster, "eminent domain is a right of a government to take private property for public use by virtue of the superior dominion of the sovereign power over all lands within its jurisdiction." In other words, if the Master has need of something, and you need it to fulfill the Master's commission, you can take it because it all belongs to Him. The earth is the Lord's and the fullness thereof.

Jesus goes into the city and into the temple and looks around. He goes back out to the Mount of Olives and prays all night. That morning on His way back to the temple, He sees a fig tree and He goes to get something to eat. Not finding any fruit on it, He curses the fig tree. The fig tree is a representation of Israel and of what Jesus is about to do. He goes back into the temple, makes a whip, and drives out the money changers, saying, *"It is written, 'My house shall be called a house of prayer,' but you have made it a 'den of thieves.'"*(Matthew 21:13). One scholar says the table Jesus turned over weighed about 2000 lbs. It was made out of stone. This was supernatural strength.

When they came out of the city, the disciples said: "Master look how quickly the fig tree withered."

Jesus tells them to have faith in God. But it can also be translated: Have the God-kind of faith. Then Jesus tells us what that is and how to operate in the God-kind of faith.

> *"For verily I say unto you, That whosoever shall say unto this mountain, Be thou removed, and be thou cast into the sea; and shall not doubt in his heart, but shall believe that those things which he saith shall come to pass; he shall have whatsoever he saith. Therefore, I say unto you,*

> *What things soever ye desire, when ye pray, believe that ye receive them, and ye shall have them*" (Mark 11:23-24).

I was with my son, Greg Jr., a missionary student at YWAM (Youth with A Mission) and he wanted to go to music school but said he had not heard a word from God. I said, "Greg, what does the Bible say? Whatsoever things you desire when you pray, believe you receive it and you shall have it. God will often lead you by the desires of your heart, because He put them there." Well, $8000.00 came in four days and Greg and his friend were off to school. We just thanked and praised God "Your kingdom come, Your will be done!"

It's All Under the Blood

The next thing God said was amazing. He said: "Forgive. If you have anything against anyone, forgive." What's that got to do with the mountain moving?

> *And when ye stand praying, forgive, if ye have ought against any: that your Father also which is in heaven may forgive you your trespasses. But if ye do not forgive, neither will your Father which is in heaven forgive your trespasses* (Mark 11:25-26).

The day will come when we will all be standing before the Father. This is what God showed me. What are you like when someone despitefully uses you or hurts you or how do you react if God leads you into a hard situation? Do you look up to heaven and cry, "Why God?" Well, until you get a revelation, you've not grown in Him. When you stand before the judgment seat and that person that did "THAT" to you is standing next to you, and you say in your heart, "Okay God, get them, go ahead and slap them, you know what they did."

And the Lord looks back at you and says, "It's all under the blood."

Then you ask, "But, Lord, aren't You even going to reprimand them?"

He says, "It's under the blood."

Then the Holy Spirit told me, "You forgot somebody."

"I did? Who?" Sitting on my shoulder was the devil whispering in my ear and accusing the brother who had hurt me.

That's when I realized, through hurt, pain and betrayal, that I had become the accuser of the brethren. I had taken on the nature of satan. Revelation 12:10- 11 says satan is the accuser of the brethren. And the day will come when we will all stand before Jesus and say, "I wish I had not done that."

And Jesus will say, "No worries, it's under the blood."

When the pastor God had led me to rejected me, I was so distraught; I didn't know what to do. I was a Catholic boy who had just started to read the Bible and believed it. I had no idea about spiritual warfare and how it works. When I talked to the pastor, I spoke faith. I thought we were on the same page, but he started talking to me about a well-known preacher from a popular church in the northeast United States. He said the preacher was operating in witchcraft and trying to speak things into existence like magic. He said, "The things that he is doing; they do in magic."

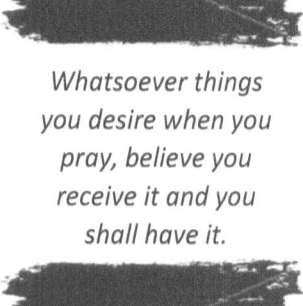

Whatsoever things you desire when you pray, believe you receive it and you shall have it.

Well, I was young, and I didn't know who the well-known pastor was, so I just agreed with him. We actually were having a faith conflict and I didn't know it. This whole time God was working behind the scenes and getting me ready for the call He had placed on my life.

During this time, I got a job working with delinquent youth. I was also attending college, and really enjoyed what I was doing. The boys and girls home I worked at was on a farm. I got Donna a job working there, too. I was the night man on Monday, Wednesday and Friday evenings. I would do a walk through the house and would always find a few boys sitting on the bench. I would approach them and ask, "What ya doing on the bench?" Well, we knew why they were on the bench." They were fighting to see "who's the baddest of them all."

In High School, I wrestled during my freshman and sophomore years. It was one of the best decisions I'd ever made. Playing football was good, but wrestling has the ability to build character, not only in me, but in those boys. So, when I came in on my shift, I would have the boys wrestle. I saw all of them mature as individuals. They grew stronger physically and mentally. I saw one boy getting pushed all over the place by the other boys, so I grabbed the toughest kid I could find, about the same weight, and had them wrestle. Well, the one boy didn't fare too well at the beginning, but after a few months, when I went to work, he would look at the other boy and say, "I'm ready for ya this time." He never did actually win, but he didn't get pinned down anymore either. That taught me something about winning: you don't always have to win to actually be the winner; just be faithful. It's not over till it's over, and God will work His plan.

For the next couple of years, I worked at this job and would go home on Sunday mornings. During this time, the pastor never called to check on me, not one time.

I graduated from Malone College and got a job at Roadway Express in Akron, Ohio. In my heart, I had really fallen away from the Lord and felt abandoned and betrayed. Why would God lead me to a pastor who would reject me like that? Well, I was about ready to get my answer.

Since Donna and I were no longer working at the boys' home, we could go to church. One of Donna's foster parents was going to a new church and it was (you guessed it!) an affiliate of the well-known preacher I mentioned previously. Over the next six or seven years, they nurtured me back to health.

While going there, I was attending a Bible class with an instructor around my age and he said something very profound to me, "Greg, God is good and the devil is bad." We were studying the book of Job and it was giving me the fits. I thought God was doing this to me and that God and satan worked together, almost like satan is God's monkey and they really are enemies, but they're plotting against me. I don't believe that way anymore. You may ask, "Wasn't God working behind the scenes to get you into the right church and get your doctrine straight?" Yes, but that was plan B. Now, it's hard to stay in some place when you are being rejected and pushed away.

A few years after I left the church, they had a large split after the pastor had just built a new church building. It was a very hard time. I started praying for the pastor and the church. God gave me a word. This would have been around 1989. The word was out of Numbers 14:9 saying, "The giants that are in your land, do not fear them, for they are bread for you and a stepping stone into the high call of Jesus Christ." If I had stayed, I could have helped that church. I failed in my assignment, because I allowed the devil to hurt me and hurt my relationship with God. But like everything satan does, it backfires. Now I know. I just have to stay on course and if you do also, God will have His way, and your love relationship with Him will grow to the point where you will be like the apostle Peter. After the first time, no matter what happened in life, Peter would never again betray Jesus.

Consequences of Pride and Fear

Look at Job, sitting on an ash heap outside his house, and scraping his flesh with a broken piece of pottery. How did Job get to this state? Job 1:8 *"And the LORD said unto satan, hast thou considered my servant Job, that there is none like him in the earth, a perfect and an upright man, one that feareth God, and escheweth evil?"* When the Lord says, *"hast thou considered...?"* we know that satan is the accuser of the saints, so we could better read this statement like this, "Satan, what is this accusation you have against my servant Job?" When the book of Job states, *"Now there was a day when the sons of God came to present themselves before the Lord, and satan came also among them"* (Job 1:6), they were not there for Thanksgiving dinner, they were in a court of law! Satan cannot do anything to you without having the legal right to do so.

Job doesn't understand that it is not God doing this to him and he pleads for an intercessor between him and God. *"O that one might plead for a man with God, as a man pleadeth for his neighbour!"* (Job 16:21). So why did all this happen to Job? In Job 41:1 God says to Job, *"Canst thou draw out leviathan with an hook?"* The Leviathan is a fire breathing dragon that lives in the sea. Job 41:34: *"He beholdeth all high things: he is a king over all the children of pride."* So pride may have been the door for all this hurt to come on Job. How did this pride get in Job to the point that satan could steal everything he had? John 10:10 *"The thief cometh not, but for to steal, and to kill, and to destroy: I am come that they might have life, and that they might have it more abundantly."* Jesus' will for you is abundant life. Satan's will is to steal, kill and destroy and everything he says is a lie; even when he is quoting Scripture, he is still a prolific liar.

It would be a very prideful thing for me to reject the healing which Jesus has purchased.

Job was serving God more out of fear and a legal obligation than out of love. This opened the door into the wrong kingdom. Job 3:25: *"For the thing which I greatly feared is come upon me, and that which I was afraid of is come unto me."* Fear and pride are brothers because you're not fully trusting God and you're not living by faith. Pride kicks in because you're trying to make it on your own, and fear kicks in because you know you can't do it on your own.

The Blood

1 John 4:18 says, *"There is no fear in love; but perfect love casteth out fear: because fear hath torment. He that feareth is not made perfect in love."* We love Him, because He first loved us. Our God loves us because that is who He is; you don't have to work for it, it's done by the blood. *"And I heard a loud voice saying in heaven, Now is come salvation, and strength, and the kingdom of our God, and the power of his Christ: for the accuser of our brethren is cast down, which accused them before our God day and night. And they overcame him by the blood of the Lamb, and by the word of their testimony"* (Revelation 12:10-11).

The blood of Jesus is the voice in Heaven that the Kingdom of God listens to. Blood has a voice as we learn in the account of Cain and Abel in Genesis 4:10: *"And he said, What hast thou done? the voice of thy brother's blood crieth unto me from the ground."* Abel's blood testified before God and God rendered judgment on Cain, who became a vagabond.

We overcome satan and his kingdom by the blood of the Lamb and the word of our testimony. The word of our testimony needs to stand in agreement with the blood. If two of us shall agree on earth as concerning anything...anything covered by the blood shall be done for us by our Father in Heaven. God loves to work on behalf of His children. The blood of Jesus has set us free because it has rendered kingdom verdicts on behalf of the blood.

Romans 8:19: *"For the earnest expectation of the creature waiteth for the manifestation of the sons of God."* Romans 8:22: *"For we know that the whole creation groaneth and travaileth in pain together until now."* Why wait for the manifestation of the sons of God? Because they have been redeemed by the Blood. Leviticus 17:14: *"...for the life of all flesh is the blood thereof."* Sometimes you need a good blood-washing. If you have an issue just pop up out of the blue, like bitterness, or you can't get over something that happened twenty years ago, you may need a good blood cleansing. Ever heard the term "hot blood"? That means something else is in control and we a good Holy Spirit blood transfusion.

> *Likewise the Spirit also helpeth our infirmities: for we know not what we should pray for as we ought: but the Spirit itself maketh intercession for us with groanings which cannot be uttered. And he that searcheth the hearts knoweth what is the mind of the Spirit, because he maketh intercession for the*

saints according to the will of God (Romans 8:26-27).

What has been purchased and redeemed by the blood? The WILL of God for the saints. Hebrews 9:12:

> *Neither by the blood of goats and calves, but by his own blood he entered in once into the holy place, having obtained eternal redemption for us. How much more shall the blood of Christ, who through the eternal Spirit offered himself without spot to God, purge your conscience from dead works to serve the living God?"*

It's all done by the blood. It's for freedom that Christ has set you free.

So what is a generational curse? Well it may take different forms, but it is a place of generational disobedience, willful or unwitting. When we obey the word and worship God according to the scripture we will always walk in victory. It is our job to stand in agreement with the blood of Jesus until we receive the purchased price of the position. That includes the nations!

Robert Henderson states in his book, ***Operating In the Courts of Heaven*** the following: "His blood is legal testimony in the courts of heaven…We are the stewards of His blood sacrifice here on earth." Wow, what a powerful responsibility God has given the church! His blood, His passion, must live in me. Jesus did not love His life. He was here for one reason and that was to redeem man, to get man back to the Father. You can't kill a dead man and the Bible states in Galatians 2:20 *"I am crucified with Christ: nevertheless I live; yet not I, but Christ liveth in me: and the life which I now live in the flesh I* *live by the faith of the Son of God, who loved me, and gave himself for me."*

That means when Christ died, my flesh died. So, I don't have to worry if I have enough faith to be healed because I'm dead. Dead men don't need faith and dead men don't complain. So when I am walking around in this flesh suit called a body, it's His faith, it's His anointing, it's His Blood that does the work. I am just a bystander enjoying the work He does through me.

The blood of the martyrs speaks volumes in Heaven. Precious is their blood. **"*Precious in the sight of the LORD is the death of his saints"*** (Psalm 116:15). Here are those ones who were beheaded for the sake of the Gospel. I only know one religion which cuts off heads, and that is Islam. *"And I saw thrones, and they sat upon them, and judgment was given unto them: and I saw the souls of them that were beheaded for the witness of Jesus, and for the word of God, and which had not worshipped the beast, neither his image"* (Revelation 20:4). These saints will rule and reign with Jesus a thousand years during His millennial reign.

> *And when he had opened the fifth seal, I saw under the altar the souls of them that were slain for the word of God, and for the testimony which they held: And they cried with a loud voice, saying, How long, O Lord, holy and true, dost thou not judge and avenge our blood on them that dwell on the earth? And white robes were given unto every one of them; and it was said unto them, that they should rest yet for a little season, until their fellow servants also and their brethren, that should be killed as they were, should be fulfilled* (Revelation 6:9-11).

I have always taught that the tribulation is an act of mercy. To me, it is better to live a few short years in hell on earth than an eternity in hell under the earth. One of the main reasons for the timing of the Tribulation is that the nations are shutting the door on the Gospel of Jesus Christ. Europe is turning churches into mosques in record numbers. Africa is being overthrown with violent Islam. Even in the Caribbean and South America there is apostasy. One of the only places I have hope for is Russia. Russia will send missionaries into Europe.

Organizations like Rick Renner Ministries have done a tremendous job when the door for the Gospel opened up in the early 1990s. The Berlin Wall came down in November 1991, but the Germans have still not embraced the Gospel. As a result, they are destroying western society as we know it. Secular humanism may embrace Islam, but Islam and especially Sharia law will never embrace western society. When the blood of the martyrs cries out, nations get saved. The blood gets power verdicts in the throne room of the court of Heaven.

5

WHEN OUR FAITH FAILS, GOD STILL WORKS

In Matthew 17 the disciples experienced a faith failure. A father brought his child to the disciples. Many say the child had epilepsy but that's just a fancy name. The child was being harassed by demons. The disciples tried to cast the demons out of him but could not. Jesus asked the boy's father, "How long has this been with him?"

"From childhood," he said. "It often throws him into the fire or into the water, trying to kill him. But if You can do anything, have compassion on us and help us."

"If you can?" echoed Jesus. "All things are possible to him who believes!"

Immediately, the boy's father cried out, "I do believe; help my unbelief!" The cry of the father is one of relinquishing his authority over to Jesus and putting his faith in Him.

In Matthew 17:21, Jesus asked the boy's father how long had this been with him. This is significant because it locates the principality or power causing the child to be tormented. Sin always invites demons. But this demon came on the boy as a child, meaning it came on him before the age of accountability. There is an age of accountability when you are twelve years old. This is when Jesus' parents found him in the temple. "Why were you looking for Me?" He asked. "Did you not know that I had to be in My Father's house?" (Luke 2:49). But they did not understand the implication of His statement. At age twelve Jesus knew it was time to participate in the family business. The age of full accountability is when you are 30. Jesus did not start his ministry until the age of 30 and this is also the time when a young man could become a Rabbi.

This boy is too young to be accountable for the demons he is battling. It may be a generational curse but that is not mentioned. Either way, the demon has no right to be tormenting that boy. And Jesus takes authority over it, casts it out and frees the boy. Praise God!

When we first started Victory Harvest Ministries of Savannah, we started in the downtown area and had a tent revival. During this time I began picking up a middle-aged woman named Elizabeth for meetings. Now, I am going to be honest with you. I thought she was partially retarded. One of her eyes was always closed and the other was about 50% open. Well, we had some on fire newly born again young women in service. And during the preaching, I felt these words come up in my spirit. "You don't have to get to some level to cast out a devil, you just have to know who you are in Christ." When I said that, I saw one woman look at the other and they both looked at Elizabeth – I said in my heart, "Oh boy, it's on now."

After service everyone left except Elizabeth, my son Aaron, one of the young ladies and me. The young lady walks behind Elizabeth, slaps a hand on her chest and says, "All right, devil, come out now!" Elizabeth's hands and feet fly straight out and she screams, "Let me go! You're killing me!"

"That's right, devil. She's going to live but you are going to die!"

After about an hour, I asked the question, "How did this devil get into this woman?"

A prophetic word came forth from the Lord. "Through abuse from childhood." No need to expound. We began to rebuke the spirit of abuse and everything else. I finally drove Elizabeth home and didn't see her till the following week. She got up and gave a testimony about what the Lord had done for her. One eye was 100% open and the other was 75% open. The lady was now articulate, speaking in complete sentences! Her IQ had jumped overnight!! The last I heard she was working in Atlanta at an old folks home. Oh, give Him praise! He's a good, good God!

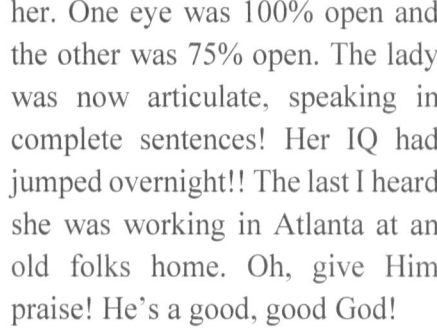

It would be a very prideful thing for me to reject the healing which Jesus has purchased.

There is more than one way to cast out a devil. One way is to do what Jesus did for this boy and Elizabeth. Others were healed or delivered as they went! Many times the Word itself will deliver a person. When I was in High School, I smoked and drank a lot. After High School I got a job at a welding shop. I had a pocket New Testament and I started reading it; as I began to memorize this scripture, I got smarter:

> *The Lord is my light and my salvation; whom shall I fear? the Lord is the strength of my life; of whom shall I be afraid? When the wicked, even mine enemies and my foes, came upon me to eat up my flesh, they stumbled and fell. Though an host*

should encamp against me, my heart shall not fear: though war should rise against me, in this will I be confident. One thing have I desired of the Lord, that will I seek after; that I may dwell in the house of the Lord all the days of my life, to behold the beauty of the Lord, and to enquire in his temple (Psalm 27:1-4).

When my son Aaron was about twelve or thirteen years old, he was preaching at a church in Savannah. The Spirit of God and the gifts of the Holy Spirit came into operation and began to reveal secret things to him. Aaron pointed his finger at a youth and said, "You can't sleep at night." The boy just looked at him, so Aaron asked, "Am I right, you can't sleep at night?" The boy just looked at him. Then Aaron said, "You've been reading Harry Potter." When Aaron said this, the boy's mother screamed. The upshot was that the boy and three quarters of the congregation came up for prayer and got delivered. If you don't play in the devil's kingdom, you won't get burned.

The Substance of Faith

Prayer and fasting builds faith to cast out devils. Mark 9:28-29: *"And when he was come into the house, his disciples asked him privately, Why could not we cast him out? And he said unto them, This kind can come forth by nothing, but by prayer and fasting."* If you pray and fast you won't have faith failures.

What is faith? Hebrews 11:1-2: *"Now faith is the substance of things hoped for, the evidence of things not seen. For by it the elders obtained a good report."* I have a very good friend, David Brooks who tells me that the substance referred to in this scripture is the death, burial and resurrection of Jesus Christ. Amen. "By faith the elders obtained a good report."

How did they do that? Through obedience. God calls those things which are not as though they were (See Romans 4:17). Just begin to praise Him for what He is about to do. Praise stills the avenger and loosens the power of God on our account.

When I was diagnosed with cancer, God gave me two Scriptures. Psalm 107:20-22: *"He sent his word, and healed them, and delivered them from their destructions. Oh that men would praise the Lord for his goodness, and for his wonderful works to the children of men! And let them sacrifice the sacrifices of thanksgiving, and declare his works with rejoicing."* The Word works and this is how you work the Word.

The other scripture God gave me was Psalm 103:5, which reads, *"Who satisfieth thy mouth with good things; so that thy youth is renewed like the eagle's."* I took my medicine. I took 35% food-grade hydrogen peroxide, and ginger root. Ginger root is hot like chemo. Food-grade hydrogen peroxide will oxygenate your blood and the oxygen will kill the cancer. I also read "The One-Minute Cure: The Secret to Healing Virtually All Diseases," which tells you how to administer it.

How did this cancer get in me in the first place? Well, I don't know, but I can tell you what I believe. My grandfather died of cancer. It started in his trachea and spread to his lungs. So, is it a generational curse? Or, could it be as the Bible says, "it rains on the just and the unjust"? I believe people get sick for a number of reasons, but the main reason is Adam sinned and the ground was cursed.

Weeds are perverted plants and cancer is perverted cells. If there is one thing I believe in life, it is the power of the corporate anointing. People get healed under the corporate anointing. I've been in a lot of services where the anointing of

God was very strong. There have been times when you could both feel and see the manifested power of God, when He displayed His presence in the room. I remember being at Rod Parsley's World Harvest Bible College; the power of God was present, and a man's ear just popped open. No one laid hands on him. There are many ways to get healed in the Bible, because people are at different levels of faith.

Let's look at another incident:

> *After this there was a feast of the Jews; and Jesus went up to Jerusalem. Now there is at Jerusalem by the sheep market a pool, which is called in the Hebrew tongue Bethesda, having five porches. In these lay a great multitude of impotent folk, of blind, halt, withered, waiting for the moving of the water. For an angel went down at a certain season into the pool, and troubled the water: whosoever then first after the troubling of the water stepped in was made whole of whatsoever disease he had. And a certain man was there, which had an infirmity thirty and eight years. When Jesus saw him lie, and knew that he had been now a long time in that case, he saith unto him, Wilt thou be made whole? The impotent man answered him, Sir, I have no man, when the water is troubled, to put me into the pool: but while I am coming, another steppeth down before me. Jesus saith unto him, Rise, take up thy bed, and walk. And immediately the man was made whole, and took up his bed, and walked: and on the same day was the sabbath* (John 5:1-9).

This is what I call gift faith. The sheep market is a representation of the church. According to Wikipedia the name "Bethesda" (ביתא/ד) is derived from the Hebrew and/or

Aramaic language and it means either house of mercy or house of grace. In both Hebrew and Aramaic, the word "hesda" could also mean "shame" or "disgrace." The location could be seen both as a place of disgrace due to the presence of invalids, and as a place of grace due to the granting of healing.

In this story, Jesus comes to a crippled man and finds he lacks faith. His only hope is, when the angel comes down and stirs the water, that some kind person would pick him up and throw him in first. Somehow that did not happen, and he blamed not being healed on his inability to get into the water fast enough. But Jesus changed the scene by telling him to "Get up! Pick up your mat and walk," and the man was instantly healed. He simply got up "picked up his mat and walked."

From Five Porches to Five Pillars

In Ephesians 4:11-13, Jesus laid out the pattern for church leadership in the early church. Here I will call it five porches or five pillars of the church.

> *And he gave some, apostles; and some, prophets; and some, evangelists; and some, pastors and teachers; For the perfecting of the saints, for the work of the ministry, for the edifying of the body of Christ: Till we all come in the unity of the faith, and of the knowledge of the Son of God, unto a perfect man, unto the measure of the stature of the fulness of Christ.*

The Apostle and Prophet

I like to compare what I call the five pillars of the church to the hand of God. It starts with the thumb. The thumb is the lowest of the fingers but it touches all the other fingers on the hand. The Apostle operates in all the other callings but he may not operate as strongly as someone who is called to a single office. For example, an Apostle may be able to preach revival, but he might not be able to do it with the fervency of the Evangelist. The Apostle, on the other hand, has a high calling to tear down satanic principalities and powers. Look at what Paul says about the calling of the Apostle.

> *For I think that God hath set forth us the apostles last, as it were appointed to death: for we are made a spectacle unto the world, and to angels, and to men. We are fools for Christ's sake, but ye are wise in Christ; we are weak, but ye are strong; ye are honourable, but we are despised. Even unto this present hour we both hunger, and thirst, and are naked, and are buffeted, and have no certain dwelling place; And labour, working with our own hands: being reviled, we bless; being persecuted, we suffer it: Being defamed, we intreat: we are made as the filth of the world, and are the offscouring of all things unto this day*! (1 Corinthians 4:9-13).

If your calling is that of an Apostle, you've got to be tough, and the Prophet is right next to him. The Prophet is the index finger and the index finger points the way. My wife has a definite prophetic anointing and I use it often. She always knows what house or car to buy. When I have an important decision to make or if I am at an impasse and don't know what to do or which way to go, I will ask my wife, and we will go with her recommendation. But sometimes it works the other way as well.

When we were getting ready to move to Savannah Georgia, we had an interesting turn of events. After Bible College, I knew God was calling us to plant a church, but I did not know where. We were in Lancaster, Ohio, and I was teaching Victory Over Darkness to new believers at the church. One of the ladies in my class said her husband did remodeling of older homes and was working in Savannah. Donna had a friend in Palmetto, South Carolina, who had asked us to come for a visit. I related it to the class I was teaching and informed them that I would miss a week from class to be on vacation. The lady said, "Oh, that's just a couple of hours from Savannah; come down and visit us." On the way there I got a prophetic word (which I referred to earlier in the book): "I'm calling you to a people you do not know, trapped in bondage by a slave mentality."

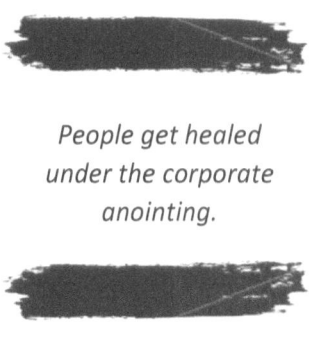

People get healed under the corporate anointing.

When we arrived in Savannah, we were driving through the town and it felt as though I was driving through a third world country. Everything was broken down! Many people from the north were just then finding out about Savannah and the entire city was being reconstructed.

Donna and I stayed in an empty apartment and slept on a blowup mattress on Hall Street right by Forsyth Park. We woke up early in the morning and walked around that Park and prayed. We went back home and put our house on the market with a realtor. Nothing moved. So, the following February, I drove back to Savannah and fasted and prayed for five days. Every time I have made a major move in my life, I did it on a prophetic word from the Lord. The fifth day arrived and still no word from God. I said in my heart, "Maybe God is talking to me differently this time." But that night I had a dream and in this dream, I met Jesus.

I was in a huge church and there were pews that were full and there were folding chairs up and down the aisle. Someone was preaching a powerful message, but I could not tell who it was because the glory cloud filled the altar. I sat down in one of the folding chairs and there was an empty folding chair just a little ahead of me. Jesus came and sat in that chair. When I first saw Him, I was surprised how young He looked. His skin had no age. He had light brown skin, light brown hair with a gold hue radiating from it, and a large Jewish nose. His Jewish features reminded me of some of my Jewish friends.

From the age of three to twelve, my family lived on Long Island in New York, and three of the families on our block were Jewish. The synagogue was right down the street, and every now and then I would go with my friends. I was raised Catholic and my parents taught me that it was Jesus who hung on the cross and died for my sins. So, whenever I walked into a Catholic Church, I knew the man hanging on the cross had died for me. I believed that and still do. In the dream, I was about to greet Jesus, but I didn't want to be rude, so I said in my heart, "I'll wait till the Preacher takes a break." Just then Jesus reached across the aisle, shook my hand and said, "It's a pleasure to meet you." When He said that, we were standing up in the glorious presence of God.

I said to Jesus, "I've given my life to You!" Then, bam! I was wide awake! I looked at the clock and it was 4:00 am, the watchman hour. I said, "Thank you, Lord. It was a pleasure meeting you." I got into my car and drove home.

I related the events of my dream to Donna. We took the house off the market with the realtor, put it up for sale by owner and raised the price by $10,000.00. A few months later the house still had not sold, but Donna had a dream. We needed the gift of the prophet to kick in, and it did. She was outside trimming the bushes when God told her, "An older couple is coming and will give you a cash deal for the house." That was about to happen but, unknown to us, we needed another move of God to get the job done.

We lived 45 minutes from World Harvest Church and we never missed a service. It was Sunday evening at 10.00 pm. Church started at 7.00 pm and Pastor Parsley gave a prophetic word. Ten dollars at ten o'clock! Then he walked off the stage. People started coming to the altar, each laying their $10 down. I just stood there. We had given thousands to the ministry and I wasn't going to do anything until I heard from God. Pastor Parsley walked back to the pulpit and said, "Ten dollars means nothing to this ministry, but you are at a prophetic moment," and he walked off the stage.

I then felt the unction and laid my $10 on the altar. This is what I call a corporate prophecy under the corporate anointing. It's up to you to grab hold of it and take it for yourself. About three days later, Donna's dream became a reality. An older couple drove up and when they did my two little kids Aaron and Victoria came running out to meet them saying, "Are you going to buy our house, are you going to buy our house?" They were jumping up and down. The house was exactly what the older couple was looking for, so they bought the house and said they needed it as soon as possible. They had just sold their florist business and offered a cash deal at asking price. They wanted to know if we would be out in a month and Donna said, "Yes, I believe we can." That's when more faith had to kick in.

6

WHEN OUR FAITH FAILS, GOD STILL WORKS
PART II

Donna had just picked up the mail and saw a local newspaper from Sheila, our contact in Georgia. So, we started looking through the housing section. She reads one off and I said, "That's our house. Take the car with Aaron and go get it." She and Aaron drove to Bloomingdale, Georgia, staying with our friends. She got things lined up with a realtor, and everything fell into place. Earlier on, I had said, "Baby, the house you circled in the newspaper, that's our house." And we have been living in it for almost twenty years. Matthew 18:19 states, *"Again I say unto you, That if two of you shall agree on earth as touching anything that they shall ask, it shall be done for them of my Father which is in heaven."*

God expects us to walk according to His Word and to operate in it. A husband and wife team speaking and saying the same thing, according to the Word of God, is one of the most powerful things on earth.

The Evangelist

The Apostle is the thumb and can touch all the other callings. But he will not be able to function as strong as someone who is just called to a specific gift like the Evangelist. I can evangelize and preach a revival message but I have also seen a lot of evangelists who can flat out preach at the drop of a hat. The evangelist is the middle finger and the longest. When they minister, souls are birthed into the kingdom of God. One of my favorite scriptures is Matthew 11:12: *"And from the days of John the Baptist until now the kingdom of heaven suffereth violence, and the violent take it by force."* The Evangelist will forcefully advance the Kingdom of God. This is demonstrated in Acts Chapter 8 when persecution comes against the church and Philip goes down to Samaria.

> *Then Philip went down to the city of Samaria, and preached Christ unto them. And the people with one accord gave heed unto those things which Philip spake, hearing and seeing the miracles which he did. For unclean spirits, crying with a loud voice, came out of many that were possessed with them: and many taken with palsies, and that were lame, were healed. And there was great joy in that city* (Acts 8:5-8).

When people truly get delivered and the power of God shows up, it is always accompanied with joy. People know Jesus is alive because of the supernatural.

In this life whenever the power of God moves, there is always going to be confrontation. Simon was a sorcerer who had bewitched the people of Samaria with his magic. He started lusting after the move of God. Not because he loved God or the people but because he loved power. Yes, satan's kingdom can give you power. Satan is the prince of the power of the air (See Ephesians 2:2). But that power is only the power of death.

Speaking in Tongues

When the disciples heard the Spirit had been poured out in Samaria, they sent Peter and John. When Peter and John got there, the move of God became even stronger and the people were filled with the Holy Spirit. When Simon saw the Spirit being poured out, he offered the Apostles money so he could administer the gift to impress all the people. The people must have been speaking in tongues as on the day of Pentecost, because devils were being cast out and healings were taking place before Peter and John even got there. This tells us a little about what God thinks about the baptism of the Holy Spirit, and the office of the Apostle. When it was just Philip in Samaria, they did miracles and unclean spirits were cast out. But when it came to the Baptism of the Holy Spirit with the evidence of speaking in tongues, they needed the anointing of Apostles Peter and John.

I have seen this in my own life. Every year a good friend of mine with a good-sized church would hold a revival. There I would always see the power of God manifested in miracles, signs and wonders. But when it came to the baptism of the Holy Spirit and the evidence of speaking in tongues, they usually sent for me. And God would show me just what to do. You get baptized in the Holy Spirit the same way you get everything else in God. You confess with your mouth and believe in your heart.

> *That if thou shalt confess with thy mouth the Lord Jesus, and shalt believe in thine heart that God hath raised him from the dead, thou shalt be saved. For with the heart man believeth unto*

righteousness; and with the mouth confession is made unto salvation. For the scripture saith, Whosoever believeth on him shall not be ashamed (Romans 10:9-11).

The Holy Spirit showed me that the first thing I should do is have them repent and ask for forgiveness. Continual repentance is a good thing. We go from one level of repentance to another level. Then I had them ask Jesus into their heart afresh so their conscience is clean. *"How much more shall the blood of Christ, who through the eternal Spirit offered himself without spot to God, purge your conscience from dead works to serve the living God"* (Hebrews. 9:14). Then I asked them to lift their hands to God and invite the Holy Spirit into their heart. Then I told them to put their hands down and explained to them, "All the gifts of God are in your belly," and I began to name the nine gifts telling them the door to operating the gifts of the Spirit is the gift of tongues.

In the book of Acts Chapter 19 the Holy Spirit gave them the unction when Paul laid his hands on them. I tell them the Holy Spirit will give you the unction but by faith you have to listen to the voice in your belly and you have to do the speaking. The Holy Spirit is not going to take control of your tongue and do the speaking for you. The Holy Spirit is a gentleman. You have a part to play. 1 Corinthians 14:32 tells us "*...the spirits of the prophets are subject to the prophets.*"

Back in 1982, when I gave my heart to Jesus Christ, I was living in a warehouse with a bunch of dudes! I was managing a rock band named Trytan led by, now a mighty man of God, Larry Dean. About this time a young woman came into my office and said: "They tell me you are saved."

I said, "Yes!"

The young woman said, "My sister says you have to speak in tongues to be saved and I want to know if that is true."

I knew I was saved but I did not speak in tongues. So I told her how I believed that it was a subsequent experience to salvation. As she walked out of the office feeling better I said in my heart. "I've got faith, I can speak in tongues." Right then I got two words. The Holy Spirit prompted me to go out and share my experience with about ten partying friends on the other side of the office. Well, I chickened out and lost my two words. After that I knew it was real and tried every way I could to get it. But I could not! Then I went to Judson College where a group of Pentecostal kids had invited a black street preacher from Chicago. He preached on the baptism of the Holy Spirit and speaking with tongues. He had the call and I could feel the power come down the line. I started talking some baby talk and said, "I didn't get it."

He said, "Yes you did, keep talking."

As I did, the manifestation got stronger and stronger and I could not stand up. I put my arms around my buddies and said, "Don't drop me." I prayed all night, filled with the power of God.

The gift of tongues is mentioned last here. Sometimes people ask me if I believe everyone should speak or pray in tongues. And the answer to that is yes. It is one of the signs of those who believe in Jesus' name. And you can either accept it or reject it. The hardest people to get filled with the Holy Spirit and the evidence of speaking in other tongues is not the new believers but the ones that have been raised in the church and have been wrongly taught.

There was a young man named Thor passing through Savannah on his BMW motorcycle. He looked like he was in his late twenties. Thor came up for prayer and gave his heart to Jesus. Then I asked Him if he wanted all of God and the baptism of the Holy Spirit with the evidence of a new prayer language in tongues. He said he did. I started praying for him and I could feel the spirits leaving his body. Then I felt the Holy Spirit say "OK." And he was gloriously filled with the power of God.

> *He that believeth and is baptized shall be saved; but he that believeth not shall be damned. And these signs shall follow them that believe; In my name shall they cast out devils; they shall speak with new tongues* (Mark 16:16-17).

There is a difference between the gift of tongues and general tongues. Similarly, there is a difference between the gift of faith and general faith or the gift of wisdom and general wisdom, or the gift of knowledge and general knowledge. The gift of knowledge starts in the present and looks back. When Jesus was in Samaria with the woman at the well and told her she had had five husbands and the one she was with now was not her husband, Jesus was operating in the gift of knowledge.

When Jesus told the disciples, "Lazarus is dead," he was operating in the Word of Wisdom which is supernatural insight into the plans and purposes of God. Even so, Jesus wept, showing compassion even though He knew He was going to raise Lazarus from the dead. This is the gift of wisdom and it is different from general wisdom. When people operate in the gift of tongues, it is different from general tongues. General tongues is for your own personal edification with God.

> *Likewise, the Spirit also helpeth our infirmities: for we know not what we should pray for as we ought: but the Spirit itself maketh intercession for us with*

groanings which cannot be uttered. And he that searcheth the hearts knoweth what is the mind of the Spirit, because he maketh intercession for the saints according to the will of God. And we know that all things work together for good to them that love God, to them who are the called according to his purpose. For whom he did foreknow, he also did predestinate to be conformed to the image of his Son, that he might be the firstborn among many brethren (Romans 8:26-29).

Oh, to be more like the Lord is my desire.

The Spirit helps our infirmities or weaknesses because we do not know how we should pray – but the Spirit does. When we pray in the Spirit or in tongues, the Holy Spirit is praying out the mysteries of God through us, making intercession according to the will of God. Jesus is seated at His intercessory position at the right hand of God, according to Ephesians 2:6: "*And hath raised us up together, and made us sit together in heavenly places in Christ Jesus.*" We are seated with Him. When? Now!

I am not an English major, but I believe the word "raised" is past tense. That means He has already done the work and we are praying out the victory He has already secured. That's what the personal gift of tongues is for. The gift of tongues is in operation, for example, when you are in a foreign country and the Holy Spirit comes on you and you begin to speak in a language unknown to you but known to others around you. It's all done as the Spirit wills.

The Pastor and Teacher

Then you have the Pastor and the Teacher. 1 Corinthians 12:27-28 "*Now ye are the body of Christ, and members in particular. And God hath set some in the church, first apostles, secondarily prophets, thirdly teachers, after that miracles, then gifts of healings, helps, governments, diversities of tongues."*

God views the teaching and preaching of the Word of paramount importance. Teaching builds faith and preaching moves the spirit. Preaching in its purest form is the spirit of prophecy. Preaching is proclamation of who God is and what He has done. The nations are not going to be won to the Lord through the teaching alone but through the anointed preaching of the Word.

When you are a pastor you have to tell people the truth that will help their relationship with the Father. A lot of times, instead of receiving correction, people will rebel and attack the pastor and this is what happened to Jesus.

Jesus helped the man at the pool of Bethesda with the gift of faith. Jesus did all the work for him. The man doesn't believe in Jesus or know who He is. Now, I really feel for Jesus, because He found the man in the temple and gives him a word and tries to help the man keep his healing. But the man betrays Jesus. What this healed man did affected Jesus' ministry! The Jews persecuted Jesus. If this man would have received correction, Jesus' life and ministry would have been easier.

> *Afterward Jesus findeth him in the temple, and said unto him, 'Behold, thou art made whole: sin no more, lest a worse thing come unto thee.'" The man departed, and told the Jews that it was Jesus, which had made him whole. And therefore did the Jews persecute Jesus, and sought to slay him, because he had done these things on the Sabbath day* (John 5:14-16).

The Jews persecuted Jesus because He healed on the Sabbath day. The Law was held in high esteem by the Jews. The early church worshiped on the first day of the week to demonstrate their freedom from the law. 1 Corinthians 16:1-2 states, *"Now concerning the collection for the saints, as I have given order to the churches of Galatia, even so do ye. Upon the first day of the week let every one of you lay by him in store, as God hath prospered him, that there be no gatherings when I come."*

Why did Paul say the first day of the week? Why not the seventh? Because they didn't worship on Saturday any longer. They worshiped on Sunday, the Lord's day, the day the Father rose the Son from the dead. Acts 20:7 states, *"And upon the first day of the week, when the disciples came together to break bread..."* So Sunday became their day of worship.

> *Christ hath redeemed us from the curse of the law, being made a curse for us: for it is written, Cursed is everyone that hangeth on a tree: That the blessing of Abraham might come on the Gentiles through Jesus Christ; that we might receive the promise of the Spirit through faith"* (Galatians 3:13-14).

Antichrist and the Coming Tribulation

It's all done by faith. When they worshiped on the first day, there was no more sacrifice for sin. The offerings are found in the book of Leviticus. That's why if you see the rebuilding of the Temple in Israel it's a big deal. Right now they are not sacrificing. There is no sin offering. That's why this is the day of Grace.

But when the temple is built, the Jews will again sacrifice for sin. The Antichrist will put a stop to it. He will cause the sacrifice to cease!

> *And he shall confirm the covenant with many for one week: and in the midst of the week he shall cause the sacrifice and the oblation to cease, and for the overspreading of abominations he shall make it desolate, even until the consummation, and that determined shall be poured upon the desolate* (Daniel 9:27).

> *And from the time that the daily sacrifice shall be taken away, and the abomination that maketh desolate set up, there shall be a thousand two hundred and ninety days* (Daniel 12:11).

From these two scriptures, we see that the tribulation is two three and a half year periods long and that the children of Israel will begin to sacrifice again. So, we must assume that the Temple will be rebuilt. In the middle of the tribulation period, the Antichrist or the Great man of peace will cause the sacrifice to cease. This is called the abomination of desolation. This is what Jesus is referring to, when Antiochus IV Epiphanes terminated sacrifice by killing a pig on the Brazen Altar during the 400 years of silence between the Old and New Testaments. Jesus said, "When you see this sign from the antichrist, run, don't go back for anything, just run" (See Matthew 24:15-21).

God has always protected Israel and He has never completely removed His protective hand over her. But when Israel begins to sacrifice for sin when Jesus already sacrificed for sin and poured His blood on the Mercy Seat, I believe the Father will say, "That is the Abomination of Desolation." It opens the door for the antichrist to walk into the Temple and proclaim himself to be the Messiah. The Jews will reject the Antichrist's claims of being the Messiah, hence his claims of being God, and they will run to the Rock called Petra. From what I understand, Petra is now being stocked with food reserves by Christians to prepare for such a time. And when they get to Petra, they will call on Jesus the Messiah and the Messiah will come. Because it was with Jesus' own blood that He purged the Sin of all men. *"Neither by the blood of goats and calves, but by his own blood he entered in once into the holy place, having obtained eternal redemption for us"* (Hebrews 9:12).

It was Ron Waytt who discovered the Ark of the Covenant. From what I understand, he was excavating in Jerusalem and went deep into the catacombs. His guide went into this one catacomb and came out screaming. Ron says he was petrified. So, he went back into the catacomb to see what scared his guide so much. He saw an angel standing next to the Ark of the covenant. On further inspection, he noticed blood on the mercy seat. Ron said, "When Jesus died and the soldier pierced him in the side with the spear, there was an earthquake. The ground split and, by divine providence, the mercy seat on the Ark of the covenant was positioned directly under where Christ had been crucified. Jesus Christ's blood penetrated through that crack in the ground and covered the mercy seat.

Ron took some of the blood and had it examined. When the scientists saw the blood, they remarked that it was dead, so there was no point examining it. But Rod insisted: "Just do it for me." So, one of the scientists put a saline solution to it and the blood became alive.

The scientist asked, "Where did you get this blood?" Ron reported that the scientist got saved after he was told where the blood came from.

Praise God! Jesus is alive! That means the healing anointing is manifest now. We have now faith and cancer must die on my faith journey!

GOD WILL USE THE FAITH OF OTHERS

Acts Chapter 3 is one of the greatest examples of the use of another's faith to heal. God still does miracles today. This is the gift of faith as well as the gift of healing in action. He's the same God today, yesterday and forever and He is a God of creative miracles!

> *Now Peter and John went up together into the temple at the hour of prayer, being the ninth hour. And a certain man lame from his mother's womb was carried, whom they laid daily at the gate of the temple which is called Beautiful, to ask alms of them that entered into the temple; Who seeing Peter and John about to go into the temple asked an alms. And Peter, fastening his eyes upon him with John, said, Look on us. And he gave heed unto them, expecting to receive something of them. Then Peter said, Silver and gold have I none; but such as I have give I thee: In the name of Jesus Christ of Nazareth rise up and walk. And he took him by the*

right hand, and lifted him up: and immediately his feet and ankle bones received strength. And he leaping up stood, and walked, and entered with them into the temple, walking, and leaping, and praising God. And all the people saw him walking and praising God (Acts 3:1-9).

What a great demonstration of the love of God!

Releasing Your Anointing

Here we see Peter and John being able to operate in the same method Jesus used. When Peter said, "*Look on us*," he created faith in the man to receive alms. But then Peter said something amazing, "*...such as I have I give unto thee: In the name of Jesus Christ of Nazareth rise up and walk.*" Peter knew what he had. Wherever Jesus went He carried the presence of God. When Jesus showed up on the scene, demons cried out, Pharisees were alarmed and the ordinary man that needed His help loved Him.

The reason most people do not operate in the miracle anointing and healing anointing of God is because they don't know what they have. It's important that you put yourself in positions where you can lay hands on the sick and watch them recover. It's all about stepping out in faith and allowing God to use you. Take fear and make it bow its knee to faith. My wife Donna and I routinely go to restaurants and she will always find someone to step out in faith and witness to. She was at a women's fellowship and prayed for a pastor's wife that had been chronically sick.

Six months later she got the report that the doctor had taken the woman off her medicine! Hallelujah, Christ is the healer! This is what happened. The lady came forward to testify of how at the last fellowship meeting, Donna prayed for a spirit of infirmity and pain to leave her. "I have been pain free every since the night you prayed for me."

God will always meet you where you are at. This is important because we see more than one of the gifts in operation. Donna had received a prophetic word of knowledge concerning a spirit of infirmity, meaning the sickness was more than physical. It was demonically inspired. The Holy Spirit had to first reveal the origin of the sickness, then the gift of healing could come into operation and then heal the woman. When this happens a refreshing comes upon the sick as God restores them.

Prophecy and Interpretation of Tongues

The nature of God is prophetic. Revelation 19:10 states that *"the testimony of Jesus is the spirit of prophecy."* The spirit of prophecy is one that *"calleth those things which be not as though they were"* (Romans 4:17). The Hebrew meaning of the phrase "to prophecy" is to flow forth, to bubble forth like a fountain, to spring forth. The Greek meaning of the words "to prophecy" is to speak for another. It includes prophetic dreams and visions.

> *Follow after charity, and desire spiritual gifts, but rather that ye may prophesy. For he that speaketh in an unknown tongue speaketh not unto men, but unto God: for no man understandeth him; howbeit in the spirit he speaketh mysteries. But he that prophesieth speaketh unto men to edification, and exhortation, and comfort. He that speaketh in an unknown tongue edifieth himself; but he that prophesieth edifieth the church. I would that ye all spake with tongues, but rather that ye prophesied: for greater is he that prophesieth than he that speaketh with tongues, except he interpret, that the*

church may receive edifying" (1 Corinthians 14:1-5).

This is the reason for tongues and interpretation of tongues, which equals prophecy. They are to edify or build up the church. Jesus usually had some type of prophetic unction before He ministered in the supernatural to someone. In Luke 13:10-17 there was a woman whom satan had bound 18 years with a spirit of infirmity. Jesus looked into the realm of the spirit and proclaimed what He saw! If you can see the invisible you can do the impossible! *"Then answered Jesus and said unto them, Verily, verily, I say unto you, The Son can do nothing of himself, but what he seeth the Father do: for what things soever he doeth, these also doeth the Son likewise. For the Father loveth the Son, and sheweth him all things that himself doeth: and he will shew him greater works than these, that ye may marvel"* (John 5:19-20). All ministry is birthed out of what the Father is doing. It's therefore important that you spend time with the Father to hear from Him.

Ecclesiastes 11:3 says, *"If the clouds be full of rain, they empty themselves upon the earth."* I believe this is a reference to one's prayer life. When your life is saturated with prayer, the supernatural begins to take over. You can always speed this up with fasting. Cornelius in Acts 10, spent time praying and fasting and he built the Jews a synagogue! That means he was a giver, and we know he had angels working for him. He just loved God.

A threefold cord is not quickly broken and that includes Praying Fasting and Giving. If you practice these three things, God will be able to enhance all facets of your life. I don't know about you, but if I have just eaten a big meal, it is very hard for me to pray in tongues. I can pray in English or sing praise songs, but I cannot pray or sing in tongues! But, if I am hungry, I can pray or sing in the spirit all day. This produces miracle breakthroughs in my life, where God is working behind the scene and controlling situations for my benefit. John G. Lake said that praying in tongues had been the making of his ministry. It was tongues and interpretation of tongues that gave him breakthrough after breakthrough.

In Spite of Everything…Rejoice!

God is the revealer of secrets. About nine months after I had been consistently cleared of lung cancer, anaplastic lymphoma kinase had died. The doctors had given me a number of Pet scans, CAT scans and MRI, which all came back cancer free. Following that, a new and deadlier form of cancer attacked my body called carcinomatosis leptomeningeal metastasis: this deadly cancer wraps itself around the bottom of the spine and chokes all communication out of the spine to the rest of the body. It hit me hard. I felt like there was a little demon standing at my right hip and grabbing hold of the nerve and pulling it. I took pain medication but nothing helped.

Finally, my wife got tired of me crying in the middle of the night and took me to the doctor. When we pulled up at the office, I told her I could not make the walk to the office, and had to use one of the wheelchairs. When the doctor saw me in a wheelchair, he had me admitted to hospital at once. They still had not found the cancer. God is always working behind the scenes.

The weekend before I went into the hospital, I found myself in north Georgia at a wedding. Donna suggested that since we were there we could go to the healing waters revival. God had spoken to Pastor Todd Smith during Christ Fellowship's 21-day fast in January, and had give him a vision of the church's baptistry. The baptism pool was full, and there was a strip of fire on top of the water.

We went to Christ Fellowship that Sunday morning but the healing waters would not open till Sunday night. We prayed about it and felt the leading of the Holy Spirit to stay. That night I was in a lot of nerve pain. A young man named Nate befriended me and helped me get to the waters. But before we went in, I said to Donna. "Come on Donna you have to go in, too. I mentioned to her one of our scriptures for the year, "You have not passed this way" and I said we may never have another chance. She ran back to the hotel and got a change of clothes. So we went into the Baptismal waters together. As soon as she was anointed with Pastor Smith's oil, she fell back into the water.

I was able to testify how God had healed me of stage four lung cancer and that the same God who healed me of lung cancer is healing me of this, too. We got out of the waters and I felt great though walking with a slight limp. Then I got dressed and we drove back to the hotel. The next day we drove back to Savannah. I still felt great, then the next two days the pain hit me. I hurt really bad and Donna sent me to the doctor; that's how I got admitted to hospital.

The day after I got there, one of the hospital doctors came to me and read me all my symptoms. He asked, "Is this happening to you?" I said "Yes." He told me that chances are it was cancer and the name is carcinomatosis leptomeningeal metastasis. The doctor was a Christian and I told him the same God that healed me of lung cancer is healing me of spinal cancer. Is anything too hard for God? So we were standing in agreement. Christ is the Healer! For the next twenty-two days, I lived my life at Candler Hospital. During this time, I learned some very important things, like continuing to speak the Word, and getting your good wife to pray you through when you are too weak to pray. God will send others to pray for you, too!

And it's not over until God says it's over. Then I was at Prophetess Karen Blackwelder's The Gathering. She oiled my head and prophesied over me: "Healing is in your inner parts; God is working in you to bring you to a place in Him that is new, a depth you never had before, a love, trust, a knowing Him. Even if there is just one at church you represent two thousand. God is dealing with stiff necks. So I said to the Lord, 'Where am I stiff-necked? He showed me and He will show you where you are stiff-necked, too.

So what did I do? I repented. I made the decision I was going to give it all to God. That means when things don't go my way, I don't get mad at God. In other words, "*Rejoice in the Lord always and again I say rejoice*" (Philippians 4:4) Notice it says "Rejoice" twice! That's the law of double enunciation, which means "God means it." God didn't get you into the mess you are in, but He will get you out of it!

PRAISE GOD IN YOUR PAIN

This is a spiritual principle that few people have been able to put into practice. But for those who are in constant pain a lot of times the praise will come through the pain. One time I was hurting real bad in my bed and my wife woke me up and said, "Greg, you've been moaning all night and I can't sleep." So we prayed and she went and slept in the back bedroom.

Keep Praising God

I was already crying, feeling alone…and then, all of a sudden, I just started singing a song and praising God. We see a lot of paradoxes in scripture, but this one was the only one I ever lived through. A paradox is a seemingly absurd or self-contradictory statement or proposition that when investigated or explained may prove to be well founded or true (Google Dictionary). Below is a paradoxical scripture concerning the Messiah.

> *Yet it pleased the Lord to bruise him; he hath put him to grief: when thou shalt make his soul an*

> *offering for sin, he shall see his seed, he shall prolong his days, and the pleasure of the Lord shall prosper in his hand.*
>
> *He shall see of the travail of his soul, and shall be satisfied: by his knowledge shall my righteous servant justify many; for he shall bear their iniquities*
>
> *Therefore will I divide him a portion with the great, and he shall divide the spoil with the strong; because he hath poured out his soul unto death: and he was numbered with the transgressors; and he bare the sin of many, and made intercession for the transgressors* (Isaiah 53:10-12).

This is the Prophet Isaiah, speaking about the 'absurdity' of what the Father has done. The opening stanza is surprising. *"Yet it pleased the Lord to bruise him. He hath put him to grief."* Why would the Father do that to the Son? The divine outcome is the glory that would follow the suffering.

> *But we see Jesus, who was made a little lower than the angels for the suffering of death, crowned with glory and honor; that he by the grace of God should taste death for every man.*
>
> *For it became him, for whom are all things, and by whom are all things, in bringing many sons unto glory, to make the captain of their salvation perfect through sufferings.*
>
> *For both he that sanctifieth and they who are sanctified are all of one: for which cause he is not ashamed to call them brethren,*

> *Saying, I will declare thy name unto my brethren, in the midst of the church will I sing praise unto thee* (Hebrews 2:10-12).

The Christian music band, Tree63, wrote a song a few years back called "Blessed Be Your Name." Some of these lyrics really capture the meaning of the above scripture.

> "Blessed be Your name. On the road marked with suffering, though there's pain in the offering, blessed be Your name."

When you're in pain, keep praising God. He didn't cause the suffering but He will deliver you of it. His very nature is redemption. Praise God!

You Are the Temple

Jesus' mission was to suffer to redeem man and bless the Father! The more I study the Word concerning the sufferings of Christ, the more I am convinced God wants me healed. God transforms man through His Word. It's the devil that comes to steal, kill and destroy. Christ came to give me abundant life! It is illegal for you to be in pain caused by the devil. Your spirit, soul and body belong to God. You are His property. Don't let the devil trespass your body, which is the temple of the Holy Spirit.

> *What? know ye not that your body is the temple of the Holy Ghost which is in you, which ye have of God, and ye are not your own? For ye are bought with a price: therefore glorify God in your body, and in your spirit, which are God's* (1 Corinthians 6:19-20).

This is an amazing scripture! It calls your body the temple of the Holy Ghost and it is given to you by God. Your responsibility is to use your body, soul and spirit to glorify God. No matter who is around or what the situation, if the Holy Ghost is alive in you, you already have the answer to every problem. And every situation will bring glory to God! Your victory was ordained before the foundation of the earth.

> *Having predestinated us unto the adoption of children by Jesus Christ to himself, according to the good pleasure of his will, To the praise of the glory of his grace, wherein he hath made us accepted in the beloved. In whom we have redemption through his blood, the forgiveness of sins, according to the riches of his grace; wherein he hath abounded toward us in all wisdom and prudence* (Ephesians 1:5).

The definition of prudence below tells us how we are to govern our bodies and our spirit once we are born again. And in order to help us we have been given the Holy Spirit with rich grace.

> *Definition of prudence* - 1: the ability to govern and discipline oneself by the use of reason. 2: sagacity or shrewdness in the management of affairs. 3: skill and good judgment in the use of resources. 4: caution or circumspection as to danger or risk.

It's our job to keep our body under discipline and God gives us His Word to do it. We are more than conquerors in the mighty name of Jesus. John 12:23-25 is the divine paradox:

> *And Jesus answered them, saying, The hour is come, that the Son of man should be glorified. Verily, verily, I say unto you, Except a corn of wheat fall into the ground and die, it abideth alone: but if it die, it bringeth forth much fruit. He that loveth his life shall lose it; and he that hateth his life in this world shall keep it unto life eternal.*

This principle is called the "Dynamics of dominion." To live you must die. The way up is the way down. To become rich, become poor. Jesus told the rich young ruler, "Go sell what you have and give it to the poor." God never gives us a resurrection that doesn't start in death; Because it's only in dying that you are born to live again.

This is why, when we praise Him in our pain, it will always produce a divine harvest and God will get the glory. All we have to do is give glory to God for seedtime and harvest! If you want to have tomorrow what you don't have today, then you have to do something today that you didn't do yesterday. And that something is sowing a seed. What kind of seed? The Holy Spirit knows.

> *I am crucified with Christ: nevertheless I live; yet not I, but Christ liveth in me: and the life which I now live in the flesh I live by the faith of the Son of God, who loved me, and gave himself for me* (Galatians 2:20).

In this life the best representation of the love of God should be our earthly father. Knowing His love gives us the faith to do the impossible. When I was in Bible College, my son Aaron was told by some bigger boys not to climb a particular tree. Later on Aaron snuck back over where the tree was and climbed it. He then fell out of the tree on a stump below, face first. It took everything he had to make it home and he collapsed in the front yard. I saw my son and went out to the front yard, scooped him up in my arms, all bloody, and I said to him, "It's going to be okay Aaron. You're going to be alright!" Aaron said at that point he knew I loved him and would not let anything bad happen to him. My son knew I loved him and would fight his battles for him. You have to feed your faith and starve your doubts to death.

The Power of Agreement

One thing that moves the Spirit is standing in agreement with other believers. And even more important is standing in agreement with God, His word and His spirit. The first person to stand in agreement with God was Himself.

> *This is he that came by water and blood, even Jesus Christ; not by water only, but by water and blood. And it is the Spirit that beareth witness, because the Spirit is truth. For there are three that bear record in heaven, the Father, the Word, and the Holy Ghost: and these three are one. And there are three that bear witness in earth, the Spirit, and the water, and the blood: and these three agree in one. If we receive the witness of men, the witness of God is greater: for this is the witness of God which he hath testified of his Son* (1 John 5:6-9).

One of the reasons I love Camp Meeting so much is because of the spirit of agreement that runs through the meetings. When this happens, you can feel the power of God in the atmosphere!

In Acts Chapter 2, on the day of Pentecost the atmosphere was supercharged with the presence of God. People were slain in the Holy Spirit. The Church stood together in agreement with God and God showed up.

> *And when the day of Pentecost was fully come, they were all with one accord in one place. And suddenly there came a sound from heaven as of a rushing mighty wind, and it filled all the house where they were sitting. And there appeared unto them cloven tongues like as of fire, and it sat upon each of them. And they were all filled with the Holy Ghost, and began to speak with other tongues, as the Spirit gave them utterance* (Acts 2:1-2).

The Holy Spirit began to speak through them and Peter preached a two minute sermon and three thousand people bowed their knees in the middle of the street and gave their lives to Jesus Christ. It also produced the healing anointing!

> *Now Peter and John went up together into the temple at the hour of prayer, being the ninth hour. And a certain man lame from his mother's womb was carried, whom they laid daily at the gate of the temple which is called Beautiful, to ask alms of them that entered into the temple; Who seeing Peter and John about to go into the temple asked an alms. And Peter, fastening his eyes upon him with John, said, Look on us. And he gave heed unto them, expecting to receive something of them. Then Peter said, Silver and gold have I none; but such as I have give I thee: In the name of Jesus Christ of Nazareth rise up and walk. And he took him by the right hand, and lifted him up: and immediately his feet and ankle bones received strength. And he*

> *leaping up stood, and walked, and entered with them into the temple, walking, and leaping, and praising God. And all the people saw him walking and praising God* (Acts 3:1-7).

What Peter and John had was Holy Spirit Power through faith in the name of Jesus.

> *And his name through faith in his name hath made this man strong, whom ye see and know: yea, the faith which is by him hath given him this perfect soundness in the presence of you all* (Acts 3:16).

"...*the faith which is by him*!" By Christ, That's the power of Holy Spirit agreement.

Spirit of the Breaker

So what happened with Ananias and his wife Sapphira? They sold their house and gave a large part of the money they received from the sale to the Church. It was so large that the Holy Spirit had to reveal it to the Apostles or they would have never known that they kept a large portion of the money for themselves. They lied to the Holy Spirit and in doing so they would have destroyed the unity of the Church. However, as a result of them dropping dead, great fear came on the Church: this is a Holy Spirit fear, and produces holiness and unity, releasing signs and wonders (Acts 5:11-12).

When this happens when the spirit of the breaker has come in:

> "*I will surely assemble, O Jacob, all of thee; I will surely gather the remnant of Israel; I will put them together as the sheep of Bozrah, as the flock in the midst of their fold: they shall make great noise by reason of the multitude of men. The breaker is*

> *come up before them: they have broken up, and have passed through the gate, and are gone out by it: and their king shall pass before them, and the Lord on the head of them* Micah 2:12-1,3)

The gate is the gate of the tabernacle, the way of salvation. But in life there are many other gates and, when you meet Jesus, He will open gates no man can shut. He is the spirit of the breaker.

2 Samuel 23:16 tells the story of David's three mighty men.

> *And the three mighty men brake through the host of the Philistines, and drew water out of the well of Bethlehem, that was by the gate, and took it, and brought it to David: nevertheless he would not drink thereof, but poured it out unto the LORD.*

The mighty men are mighty men because of association! They had been in a cave with a giant killer, whose name was David. And during this time a transformation took place in the hearts and minds of these men: they themselves became giant killers like David. Their life went from a life of need to a life of abundance and victory!

> *David therefore departed thence, and escaped to the cave Adullam: and when his brethren and all his father's house heard it, they went down thither to him. And every one that was in distress, and every one that was in debt, and every one that was discontented, gathered themselves unto him; and he became a captain over them: and there were with him about four hundred men* (1 Samuel 22:1-2).

> *Moreover the Philistines had yet war again with Israel; and David went down, and his servants with him, and fought against the Philistines: and David waxed faint. And Ishbibenob, which was of the sons of the giant, the weight of whose spear weighed three hundred shekels of brass in weight, he being girded with a new sword, thought to have slain David. But Abishai the son of Zeruiah succoured him, and smote the Philistine, and killed him. Then the men of David sware unto him, saying, Thou shalt go no more out with us to battle, that thou quench not the light of Israel* (1 Samuel 21:15-17).

As David got older, he lost a step or two, so the men associated with him had to fight for him. He was the king and a mighty warrior, who had trained his mighty warriors. They would now take care of him.

When I was diagnosed with lung cancer the news was hard on the family, but behaviorally it was not so bad because I could do everything I could before. When the spinal cancer hit me, I became a cripple and spent close to four weeks in the hospital. When I left the hospital, I could only walk 200 feet at a time. I was not stable and had to use a walker. Some places I went I needed a wheelchair. It was a big adjustment for my family, but they stood by me. We bound our faith together and spoke God's word, praising Him for the victory in advance!

I heard one preacher say that during the revolutionary war our forefathers first declared the victory and then fought the war. And that's why I believe we received the victory in fighting lung cancer and I am continually getting stronger while fighting spine cancer. The Bible declares it will not return a second time: *"What do ye imagine against the Lord? he will make an utter end: affliction shall not rise up the second time"* (Nahum 1:9).

The spinal cancer that has been afflicting me is an illegal occupant and must die, in the mighty name of Jesus. The Spirit of the breaker always brings freedom.

> *Now the Lord is that Spirit: and where the Spirit of the Lord is, there is liberty. But we all, with open face beholding as in a glass the glory of the Lord, are changed into the same image from glory to glory, even as by the Spirit of the Lord* (2 Corinthians 3:17-18).

As we move from glory into deeper glory the substance of faith becomes self evident. Faith stands in the gap until the manifestation shows up. Faith is the exact image of what you are hoping for. Faith is the image of things that you have hoped and prayed for.

Covenant Is Forever

The story of Mephibosheth is a wonderful illustration of the mercy of the Lord and how God the Lord of the breakthrough will reach down to needy children. Mephibosheth was the son of Jonathon and King Saul's grandson. Both Saul and Jonathon died in battle against the Philistines. Mephibosheth's caretaker, expecting the palace to be overrun by enemies, picked up Mephibosheth and started running. But she fell on the child, and as a result he was crippled in both his feet.

Years later he was living down in Lodebar, which means no pasture, a land of nothing, a place where making a living is hard. But one day King David remembered his love and the covenant he cut with Mephibosheth's father, Jonathan.

King David asked, "Is there anyone left in the house of Saul I can bless?" One of David's servants, Ziba, left over from King Saul's dynasty told him about Mephibosheth. David orders that Mephibosheth be brought to the palace. He is summoned before the King.

Samuel 9 describes the meeting of Mephibosheth and King David. The young man humbly bows before the King and David tells him to not be afraid. David bestows a blessing on Mephibosheth saying: "I will surely show you kindness for the sake of your father Jonathan. I will restore to you all the land that belonged to your grandfather Saul and you will always eat at my table" (2 Samuel 9:7). Mephibosheth bowed and asked why David would "notice a dead dog like me?"

At this point the king would have reached out his hand toward the young man and Mephibosheth would have seen the scar! That scar was caused when his father had cut covenant with David, the now reigning king. Mephibosheth is in covenant with the king because of his father and he did not even know it. But now he is receiving the blessing. He didn't have to work for it; he only had to receive it.

About the Author

Pastor Greg Van Gorp has been married to Donna M. Strosnider Van Gorp since December 27, 1987. They have two sons, two daughters, and a beautiful granddaughter, Elise.

Pastor Greg graduated with honors from World Harvest Bible College, known today as Valor Christian College. The college is located in Canal Winchester, Ohio, and Pastor Rod Parsley serves as the senior pastor. He proceeded to obtain his license to preach at LeSea Ministries, and in August 2002 was ordained a preacher by Pastor Rod Parsley of World Harvest Church.

In February 1998, when crossing the Talmadge Memorial Bridge to visit friends, Pastor Greg felt God speaking to him about the city of Savannah, GA:

> I am taking you to a people you do not know, who are in bondage to a slave mentality brought in by a Spirit of Voodoo. Later he heard, *"I am calling you to turn the hearts of the fathers to their children, and the hearts of the children to their fathers* (Malachi 4:6).

In obedience, the Van Gorp family moved to Bloomingdale, GA, to answer the prophetic call to Savannah. And so, in October 2000, Victory Harvest Ministries of Savannah, Inc. was birthed. Pastor Greg began working in construction, while conducting personal street ministry in downtown Savannah and assisting local jail ministries. Donna edited their weekly TV shows to be aired at Bethesda, Coastal Video Productions, while homeschooling their four young children.

The work of Victory Harvest Ministries began in the inner city reaching out to the lost and imparting hope to believers. They held their worship services in a store-front office building in Inner City Savannah until 2006.

Pastors Greg and Donna trained inner city children in dance and drama and held tent & healing revivals with local ministers. They taught marriage and women's ministry seminars and held breakfast fellowships to encourage local pastors, as well as traveled with their twelve-year-old son, Evangelist Aaron Van Gorp.

In December 2007, the ministry planted a financial seed of $2777.77 as a Resurrection seed offering, believing for its own building. That miracle came in October 2010 with a donation of fourteen acres of land and half a million dollars to build. And so, in January 2014, Harvest Time Church, a branch of Victory Harvest Ministries of Savannah, Inc., opened its doors for service.

Since 2015 God has called Pastor Greg and Pastor Donna to Apostleship, providing covering to ministers through licensing & ordaining. They led a mission team to Calabar, Nigeria, to train Bible College students and distribute food to undernourished children. They are also active in outreach revivals and special events monthly to equip the body of Christ and to reach the lost.

For more information, visit:
www.harvesttimesavannah.com

www.ingramcontent.com/pod-product-compliance
Lightning Source LLC
Chambersburg PA
CBHW021116080526
44587CB00010B/539